■ LETTERS

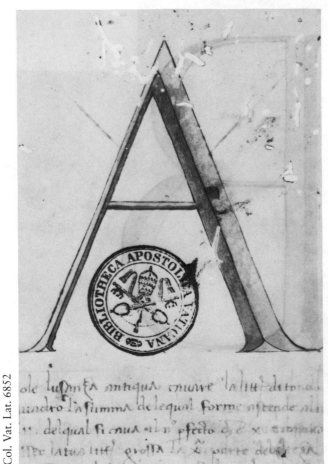

Drawing by Felice Feliciano, c. 1463.
Bibliotheca Apostolica Vaticana.
Col. Vat. Lat. 6852

LETTERS

■

JAMES HUTCHINSON

Professor of Graphic Communications
California Polytechnic State University
San Luis Obispo

 Van Nostrand Reinhold Company
New York Cincinnati Toronto London Melbourne

PRINTED IN THE UNITED STATES OF AMERICA
DESIGNED BY THE AUTHOR

PUBLISHED BY VAN NOSTRAND REINHOLD COMPANY INC.
135 WEST 50TH STREET
NEW YORK, NEW YORK 10020

VAN NOSTRAND REINHOLD
480 LATROBE STREET
MELBOURNE, VICTORIA 3000, AUSTRALIA

VAN NOSTRAND REINHOLD COMPANY LIMITED
MOLLY MILLARS LANE
WOKINGHAM, BERKSHIRE RG11 2PY, ENGLAND

16 15 14 13 12 11 10 9 8 7 6 5 4 3 2 1

LIBRARY OF CONGRESS CATALOGING
IN PUBLICATION DATA

HUTCHINSON, JAMES.
　LETTERS.

　BIBLIOGRAPHY: P.
　INCLUDES INDEX.
　　1. WRITING–HISTORY. 2. ALPHABET–HISTORY.
3. PRINTING–HISTORY. I. TITLE.
Z40.H87 1983   001.54'3   83-1185
ISBN 0-442-23267-5 (cl)

INTRODUCTION 9

ACKNOWLEDGMENTS

This book is intended as a brief discussion about the development of letterforms before and since the advent of movable type, as related primarily to typography. It is an elaboration of several lectures incorporated in a course I teach about typographic principles, practice, and design.

The aim of this book is to present a broad view of the interrelation of alphabetic characters used on a page, from a lost and distant past to the present. In presenting this view, I had to make the choice of using a technical form available to specialists within the field or a form which was understandable and helpful to persons not only in typography, but to those in allied fields such as graphic design and art. I've chosen the latter.

In writing the book, my obligations to the authors of published studies of alphabetic writing and typographic history are numerous. There are a number of excellent books about specific periods, particularly Jensen's Sign, Symbol and Script, Gelb's A Study of Writing, and Updike's Printing Types: Their History, Forms, and Use. I'm indebted to them, and to the writings of many others as well, some of whom are cited in "References." None of the authors whose works I've drawn on is to be held accountable for the liberties I've taken in the restatement, application, and modification of their views.

Thanks are due to the following libraries and museums, for permission to reproduce exhibits of early writing and pages from rare books and manuscripts in their collections.

The Pierpont Morgan Library, New York
The Metropolitan Museum of Art, New York
The Huntington Library, San Marino
The Bodleian Library, Oxford
The British Library, London

Bibliotheca Apostolica Vaticana, Vatican City
Museo Nationale Etrusco, Rome
Oesterreichische Nationalbibliothek, Vienna
Bayerische Staatsbibliothek, Munich
Kunstgewerbemuseum, Berlin
Bibliotheque Nationale, Paris
The Louvre, Paris

I'm indebted also to the rare books and manuscripts
divisions of The New York Public Library and The Pierpont
Morgan Library, for permitting me to study many of the
magnificent books and manuscripts in their collections.

For help with many technical details, I wish
to gratefully acknowledge the indispensable assistance
of Michael Clarke and Michael Farmer, who set the type,
and Gary Valente, whose photographic help was creative
and continuous. Similarly, I'm indebted to Steve Byers,
Director, Typographic Division, Mergenthaler Linotype
Company, for exhibits of digital typefaces he had set
for me; and to Robert Lucas, for translations from Latin
texts.

A like note of appreciation must go to Professors
Eugene Coleman and John Wordeman, my friends and
colleagues, who have taken an interest in this project and
have played a role in its completion.

J.H.

TO MY WIFE, LORETTA,
AND MY DAUGHTER AMY

HRONM

P LURES FUISSE
QUI EUANGELIA
SCRIPSERUNT
ET LUCAS EUAN
GELISTA TESTAT
DICENS. QNM QUI

dem multi conati sunt ordinare narrationem

rerū quae in nobis complexe sunt sicut tradiderunt

nobis qui ab initio ipsi uider sermonem et ministra

uerunt ei. Et per seuerantia usq: ad presens tempus

monimenta declarant quae adiuersis auctorib;

edita diuersarū hæresiū fuere principia. ut ea ill

iuxta aegyptios et thomæ et matthiæ et bard

lomeūm duodecim quoq: aptorū et basilidis atqu

apellis ac reliquorū quos enumerare longissimū

Cum hoc tantū in presentiarum necesse sit dicere ea

tasse quosdam qui sine spū et gratia di conati sunt

magis ordinare narrationem. quam historiæ

Gospels in Latin. An example of letterforms from the monastery
of St. Martin at Tours, France; between 857 and 862.
The Pierpont Morgan Library, New York. M 860, fol.4v.

INTRODUCTION

The shapes of the letters you are reading were modeled on Roman letters. The earliest Roman printing types were introduced in Italy during the Renaissance and were a revival of the lettering

multa fagaciores acutioresq; fint: Nam de Aegyptiis dicere oporteat: bæluas enim & ferpétes & uiuos & mortuos Hæc igitur ifpiciés diuinus ille uir mœnibus ferreis & a cæteris gétibus fepare nos uoluit: quo pacto facilius corpore imaculatos lógeq; ab huiufcemodi falfis opinioïbus remotos bat: ut folū uerū deum præter cæteras gentes adorantes illi

Type design of Nicholas Jenson, 1470.

in which classical learning had been preserved during the reign of Charlemagne. This antique lettering preserved in a calligraphic revival of the ninth century was in part a return

Carolingian minuscule, 798-99.

to early Roman characters which go back to the Christian era.

In tracing the ancestry of Roman letters, we realize that the first printed books were imitations of late manuscripts.

Type faces used today are

terrestre certamen.

pro decore et utilitate

propter necessitatem

Humanist book hand, c. 1450.

9

historically tied to the first printing types,
and the first types were connected to the letters
formed by the calligraphers' manuscript book hand
in Latin.[1] The Latin alphabet was a development
from a similar source as the Greek alphabet,
which was an adaptation of a writing among the
Semites of Syria in about 2500 B.C. This Semitic
writing can't be traced, but its principles
are those of the Egyptian system of written signs
representing spoken syllables. That part of the
Egyptian system of writing belonged to ancient
methods of writing, and the oldest of these
writings, Sumerian, has been followed from
about 3000 B.C.

So writing was the result of a slow and
natural development over thousands of years.
It may have begun with cave paintings, or
cuneiform marks, or hieroglyphics. No one knows.
We do know, though, that civilization – which
couldn't exist without writing – didn't develop
in the same way and at the same time among all
peoples, and the same was true of writing.
But it seems to be generally accepted that
practically all writing started with pictures.

In picture writing, the emphasis was on
the picture or symbol. The meaning could be

C. 12000 B.C. ■ Prehistoric pictures requiring brushes to render them
were painted by Cro-Magnon cave dwellers on walls at Dordogne.

expressed orally in any language. Picture writings weren't necessarily similar or sequential in their development by ancient peoples, the prehistoric inhabitants of Mesopotamia, Egypt, Phoenicia, Europe and other places, or by more recent peoples.

Picture writing evolved in two stages. The first was pictographic; the second was ideographic.

A pictogram was a picture or symbol that represented the object or thing shown.

(It could be called a petrogram if it were drawn or painted; a petroglyph if it had been cut or carved in stone. But for our purposes, pictograms include all.) An ideogram (or, perhaps to be more precise, a logogram) was a picture or symbol that represented, by suggestion, an idea associated with the thing depicted. It stood for one or more words.

A pictogram represented nothing more than the object it portrayed. If a circle were drawn to express sun, that was a pictogram. A pictogram would have become an ideogram if it had no longer represented the object depicted, but an idea (or a word or words) associated with the object. For example, when the drawing mentioned before no longer signified sun, but light or heat or day, it became an ideogram.

The difference between a pictogram and an ideogram hasn't been clearly defined. The line of demarcation between them was very faint, in many instances, because pictograms gradually evolved into ideograms. Because of differences among scholars about whether a particular pictorial sign should have been termed a pictogram or ideogram, or the appropriateness of these terms to define early ways of writing, the term "representational writing" is considered more appropriate by some and a better name for picture writing in general.[2]

Picture writing (or representational writing, if you prefer) went through a series of steps in its development. In time objects were represented by a minimum of strokes that assumed a simpler and also more stylized form.[3] The symbol for man, although it varied with different peoples, was generally reduced to a stick figure.

Picture writers found that they could express different things and give character to their pictures by adding characteristic features. A man with a cane would represent an old man.

Simplified pictures had a serious disadvantage.

C. 4500 B.C. ■ Ideograms, written and still used by the Chinese, appeared.

They could represent things which could be seen,
but to represent what could not be seen was, on occasion,
impossible or more difficult.

More complete stories became possible with
idea-pictures, which were used side-by-side with pictograms
for centuries.

Picture writing had another disadvantage.
Pictures could be drawn differently by different writers,
and the writers didn't always use the same symbols
or pictures for each idea or thing. The circle symbol
for <u>sun</u> might be used by one writer to mean <u>day</u>,
and by another to stand for <u>light</u>.

As civilizations grew and society became more
complex, greater ingenuity was needed to devise new
idea-pictures. Some peoples advanced slowly
to the final step where picture writing
developed into sound writing by means of
syllables or letters. That isn't to say that
writing naturally progressed through stages
which were mutually distinct, or that people
abandoned their picture writing when
the alphabet was developed. Pictures, of course,
are still used, because they can often tell as much
or more very simply.

After picture writing came phonetic
writing. Its ancestry may have begun with the
Egyptians. It should be noted, though, that the
Mesopotamians and the Cretans, who attained
cultural and commercial civilizations that

rivaled those of the Egyptians, could have exerted an influence.[4]

The possible ancestry of our alphabet can be exhibited by showing the evolution of the letters from people to people. Take, for example, the letter <u>A</u>. The Egyptian sign for an eagle stood for an <u>a</u> sound in a proper name. The Phoenician (Old North-Semitic) name for A was 'aleph, which meant "ox," and the form of their letter may have had a Babylonian or Egyptian origin — the Babylonian sign for "ox" was ; the Egyptian hieroglyph for "cow" was (The Sinai script was variations on or .) The early Greek name was alpha. The Etruscans adapted a symbol similar to the early Greek one, and the Romans changed it to the letter .

The Babylonians and Egyptians didn't develop an alphabet in which each sign stood for a sound. They did add signs of purely phonetic value to their ideograms. They developed writing systems which were a combination of idea-writing and sound-writing, which was a significant advancement.

Apparently, true phonetic writing was a Semitic invention. Perhaps the Egyptians brought their system of writing to the Sinai Peninsula, and ancient Semites improved upon the Egyptian way of writing.

The system of writing which the Semites developed contained two dozen consonant letters. From Sinai this alphabet might have been carried by immigrants or tradesmen through Palestine to the Northwest Semitic Phoenicians. The Phoenicians may have been influenced by the scripts of other peoples, but the Sinaitic origin of their alphabet might be reasonable. [5]

Our alphabet made its way from the Phoenicians to the ancient Greeks, who added the vowels. From Greece the letters may have crossed the Mediterranean Sea to the Etruscans, who were the dominant power in Italy about a thousand years before Christ. Or, the Etruscans could have received their alphabet from a similar source as the Greeks. From the Etruscans, the earliest forms of the Roman alphabet were saved, and those shapes provided the immediate source of the capital alphabet we use.

Picture writing
Phonetic or sound writing

Mesopotamian	Egyptian	Aegean
	▪	▪
	Proto-Semitic	Cretans
	(Sinai)	
	▪	
	Phoenician	
	(Northwest Semitic alphabet)	
	▪	
	Greek	
	▪	
	Etruscan	
	▪	
	Roman	

1 NON-ALPHABETIC WRITING

We know not when, and we cannot guess where,
there dawned upon some mind the fact that all the words
which people uttered are expressed by a few sounds.
Hence, what better plan than to select
from the big and confused mass of ideograms,
and all their kin, a certain number of signs
to denote, unvaryingly, certain sounds?
That was the birth of the alphabet, one of the greatest
and most momentous triumphs of the human mind.

Edward Clodd

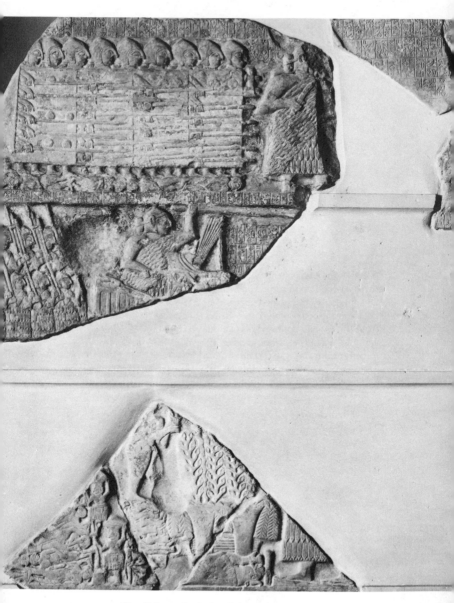

Detail from the Stele of the Vultures (fragment).
Mesopotamia, the first half of Third Millennium B.C.
Limestone, total height of 74 inches. The Louvre.

MESOPOTAMIAN CUNEIFORM SCRIPTS

Civilization developed in Mesopotamia, now called Iraq,
over five thousand years ago. It first appeared
in the south near the Persian Gulf, where the country
of Sumer was located. Later, Babylon to the north
dominated.

In the deserts of Mesopotamia, mounds
or tells were found in which were unearthed the ruins
of ancient cities. Among the broken pottery, household
utensils, and other discoveries were bricklike tablets

with small wedge-shaped marks.

Apparently the tablets had been written on wet
clay, baked in furnaces, and dried in the sun.
In time, the marks were recognized as a
system of writing called cuneiform, and told
about the civilization and what happened there
about 3,000 B.C.

It seems the cuneiform script was handed down
to the Babylonians from the Sumerians. Whether or not
the Sumerians started it isn't known.

The Sumerians moved into southern Mesopotamia
and founded the first civilization there. Writing was
used by them at first for keeping records. Since

paper and parchment didn't exist, the Sumerians used mainly clay to write on. Scribes drew pictures which represented objects on the soft clay with a piece of reed having one end cut to an edge.

Ancient Ideogram	Old Babylonian Cuneiform Script	Meaning
		fish
		ox

Picture-signs could be compound as well. The sign for "wild ox" was made up of the signs for "ox" and "mountain."[1]

Later, they used pictures to represent ideas suggested by the picture. The rising sun could stand for day.

Representative pictures, however, were difficult to draw on wet clay. To draw a line, a scribe would press a stylus a number of times into the soft clay. Since the stylus was held at an angle, one end went deeper, leaving a wedge-shaped impression.

The wedges were pressed in an up-and-down, horizontal, and an oblique manner. In addition, the tip of the stylus was used, making a mark like an arrowhead.

C. 2500 B.C. ■ The first inks used in early Chinese and Egyptian civilizations were made of lampblack ground with a solution of glue or gums. The mixture was made in stick form and dried. Before they were used, the sticks were mixed with water.

So just these four kinds of marks were used to create all pictures, resulting in pictures which lost their resemblance to the objects from which they originated. [2] The picture-sign (hieroglyph) for "sun" was a diamond-shaped figure which later became , and the latest cuneiform . [3]

Also, a cuneiform sign could have more than one meaning. The same sign could stand for a syllable, a whole idea, a word by itself, or a proper name. To facilitate reading, scribes placed signs called determinatives next to the word sign to help the reader understand the meaning of the word.

Although the number of determinatives that occurred in the cuneiform script was small, it was customary to place before the names of people and occupations a sign for "human, man;" after names of places and countries a sign for "place," and so on. [4]

The Babylonians took over the Sumerian writing and used it for their own language. The signs meant a whole word, a syllable, or the vowels a, e, i, and u. Consequently, the Babylonians never had an alphabet; they used a system of writing with more than 350 signs. [5]

Cuneiform, it seems, wasn't a direct ancestor of the alphabet. But some scholars say that the Sumerians first invented writing and the Egyptians borrowed the idea from them, producing their own system.

Detail from Stele of the Serpent King, Egypt, Abydos, c. 3000 B.C. Limestone, height 56 inches. The Louvre.

EGYPTIAN SCRIPTS

Like the Babylonians and others, the Egyptians tried
to record events with pictures. Simple pictures, as said
earlier, weren't always able to communicate the same
message to everyone. Also, there were limits to the
complexity of the messages that pictures could convey.

An early stage in the development
of picture-writing was abstraction. Objects
such as a swallow, were represented in simple,

stylized outline drawing. To

represent a visible action or an abstract
concept, the Egyptians, like others, created
ideograms or idea pictures. The association of
ideas was introduced and pictures were chosen
which related to the idea to be shared.

So "to cry" was depicted by an eye

with tears; "to find" was represented by a

pecking ibis .

Later, the Egyptians recognized the
relationship between the visual sign and the
spoken word for the same thing. The sound made
when pronouncing a word was as much a symbol

for the thing as the simplified drawing. The difference, of course, was that one was seen and the other was heard. When the association became clear, the written sign could be read aloud, and it ceased to be a picture; it became a sign that represented the spoken word.

As a consequence, the Egyptians represented a word by a picture that denoted an object of the same phonetic character, by means of a rebus. For instance, the hieroglyph of a swallow was w̱r in the language– pronounced with a certain vowel sound that isn't known. In time, the sign was used for another word that had the same pronunciation but a different meaning; w̱r meant both "swallow" and "big." At this stage, the pictorial origin of the symbol wasn't important; the sign stood for a certain sound.

In the Egyptian language, there was a predominance of consonants over vowels. Vowels simply modified the main concept expressed through the consonants. Therefore, their language had a large number of homonyms, in the sense of words having the same consonants.[6]

Pairs of words that sounded alike but had different meanings were limited, and other ways for writing the remaining words had to be created. In so doing, they discovered the principle of the alphabet–that words could be split up and written with separate signs for each

(consonant) sound. A strip of cloth was s̱

(followed by an unknown vowel); lake was

sh. By using these and other signs for the sounds
with which they said the words, the Egyptians
had the basis of an alphabet.

ACROPHONY

There weren't enough words of one syllable
for all of the consonantal sounds of their
language. To fill in what was missing, they
used a method called acrophony. A sound was
indicated by the use of a picture or the name
of something that began with the sound
they wanted.

Object	Picture-Sign	Name	Sound Value
hand		derct	d
mouth		ro	r

With the help of acrophony the Egyptians developed
24 symbols, each of which signified one particular sound.
When so used, these signs had the character of letters.
Some of the signs, unfortunately, differed for the
same letter. It appeared that the scribes did not spell
the same way all the time. Nevertheless, the signs
included all the consonants of the Egyptian language
and could be considered a kind of alphabet.

Object	Picture Sign	Sound Value
vulture		'
reed		j
forearm		'
quail		w
leg		b
seat		p
horned snake		f
owl		m
water		n
mouth		r
courtyard		h

coiled flax		ḥ
unknown		kh
animal's stomach		
bar or bolt		s
folded cloth		
sea; lake		sh
hill		q
basket		k
jug stand		g
bread		t
animal halter		th
hand		d
snake		ds, dj

The system couldn't be considered a complete alphabet, though; it showed only the consonants and not the vowels. (Like most of the Semitic writing systems, Egyptian never had vowels. The readers had to provide the vowels according to the context.)

When the Egyptians adopted signs to represent each consonantal sound in their ancient writing, it was possible for them to write every word with only 24 signs, as we do with 26 letters. This final step wasn't taken by them, however. They maintained over 3,000 hieroglyphic signs; at least 300 to 400 of them were in regular use and were needed for reading.

Pure phonetic writing could have brought some disadvantages, though; there was a large number of words in their language of the same consonantal structure. Ambiguity was removed in many instances by adding another symbol, as the Sumerians had devised— a word sign that was written but not spoken. These determinatives were intended to explain the meaning of the written word. For example, the word mnh could mean papyrus plant, youth, or wax. If it were to mean a papyrus plant, a determinative for the general

category of "plants", was added to the phonetic

spelling. Also, a determinative could have given a more precise naming to a word.

Some common determinatives were (men), (women), (trees), and (light).

Hieroglyphic writing of the Egyptians was used largely for ornamental purposes and appeared on temple walls, in tombs and other

buildings. Hieroglyphs ("glyphein," to carve) were rendered in the form of a low or high relief, often in color. They were chiselled in stone mainly, and the forms were incised or in relief. When the Egyptians developed papyrus, they had a paper-like surface that could be written on with a pen or a sort of brush. Writing with the reed pen produced a simplified form of the earlier picture letters. The materials and the desire for faster writing brought about a new style of writing around 3500 B.C. The new system of symbols, based on the hieroglyphs, was called <u>hieratic</u>. Although its use was restricted to recording religious literature at first, it came to be used for nearly all writing, except monumental records.

A third style of writing, which was simpler, was called <u>demotic</u> (popular). It was used in trade or commerce. Its use began about 900 B.C. and continued to the fourth century.

Hieroglyph	Hieroglyphic Book Script	Hieratic	Demotic

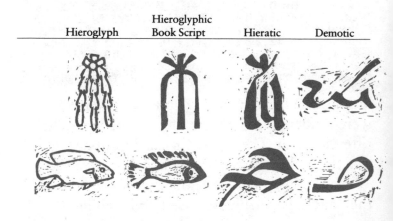

PHOENICIAN
AND OTHER OLD NORTH-SEMITIC SCRIPTS

Credit for making the last step toward a writing system without the use of pictograms, ideograms, and determinatives has been given to the Semites. "Semites" refers not to a particular people, but to many peoples who spoke Semitic languages, and who lived on the land between Mesopotamia and Egypt. Presumably, they were influenced by both civilizations, and perhaps others.

The Phoenician coastal strip was the land route between Asia and Africa; its shore connected the sea routes of Europe with Asia and Africa. Its geographic position and trade provided for a mingling of cultures, and the Phoenicians apparently borrowed and benefited from all of them.

How and when the Phoenician alphabet came into being hasn't been determined. Important discoveries and inscriptions from 2000 to 800 B.C., located in the area of Sinai, Palestine, and Syria, provide some guidelines about the history of the development of alphabetic writing.

BYBLOS SCRIPT

A kind of writing that hadn't been known before

was discovered at the port city of Byblos
at the base of the Lebanon Mountains. The writing
resembled Egyptian and was thought to be syllabic.
Believed to have been written about 2000 B.C.,
it showed an early attempt to create a new system
of writing.

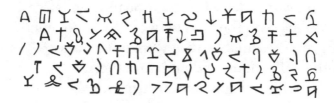

The people who lived in Byblos, the other seaport
cities at the base of the Lebanons, and their
immediate neighbors beyond the mountains
spoke a common language. Their words were
made up of sounds for consonants; the vowels
were considered unimportant. So each word was
a particular combination of consonant sounds.
N'n was the sound combination for nun (fish);
m'm was for mem (water). Neither n'n or m'm
was used for anything else.

The words of the Phoenicians were difficult
to present in the picture manner of the Egyptians.
Longer words weren't made from simple object-names
placed side by side, one after the other. Rather,
they were developed by adding extra consonant sounds.

For example, we can make up in English a word like "pressman," in which the parts are words in themselves— "press" and "man." More often, though, the added part isn't a word, as in changing "print" to "printer." We can't picture "er" since it isn't an object. Similarly, the picture method wouldn't work for longer Phoenician words.

The Phoenicians worked out a modified picture display arrangement around 1300 B.C. The picture of a fish, for instance, was used not for their word for fish, <u>nun</u>, but just for the first consonant sound in the word. The whole word was shown by two fishes in a row—one of each <u>n</u> sound. [7]

Each of their 22 consonant sounds was worked out. Then an object that had a particular sound at the beginning of its name was chosen for each sound. Next a simple and distinctive picture of each object was designed (for brush handling on papyrus). Finally, the names and designs were made into a list for memorizing.

Object	Picture Sign	Name	Sound Value
ox	𐤀	'aleph	'
house	𐤁	beth	b
stick, camel?	𐤂	gimel	g
door	𐤃	daleth	d
window ?	𐤄	he'	h
hook	𐤅	waw	w

Object	Picture Sign	Name	Sound Value
weapon	⅃Ξ	zajin	z
fence?	ⴸĦ	kheth	h
bale?	⊗	teth	t
hand	⟋	jodh	j
palm of hand	ϒ	kaph	k
ox-goad?	⎿	lamedh	l
water	ⳘϞ	mem	m
fish	⟋⟋	nun	n
support?	⟊	samekh	s
eye	O	'ajin	'
mouth	⅃	pe	p
fishhook?	⋔	sadhe	s
monkey?	ⴲ	qoph	q
head	ⴹ	resh	r
tooth	W	sin	sh
mark, sign	X	taw	t

UGARIT ALPHABET

At Ras esh-Shamra, the site of ancient Ugarit,
a large number of clay tablets were discovered.
The discovery established that the Phoenicians
of ancient Ugarit had created a simple alphabet

about 1400-1200 B.C. that used cuneiform signs. One small tablet had inscribed on it not over 30 signs that ran from left to right, a purely alphabetic system without ideograms or determinatives. Twenty-seven of the signs were the usual Semitic kind which expressed a consonant plus any vowel. Three, though, signified 'a, 'i, and 'u. [8] The sequence of letters fixed the traditional order which the Hebrews, Greeks, and Romans inherited.

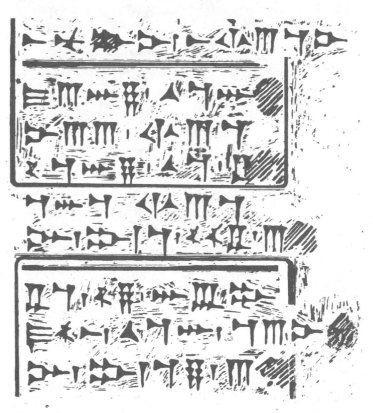

Their alphabet didn't have any connection
with the cuneiform system of writing except
that the signs were impressed in a similar way
with a stylus on clay. Apparently, the scribes
at Ugarit adapted the wedge-shaped marks to their
own Phoenician alphabet, for writing on clay. [9]

Sign	Sound Value	Sign	Sound Value
	'(a)		d
	b		n
	g		z̧
	h		s
	d		'
	h		p
	w		ṣ
	z		q
	ḥ		r
	ṭ		'(i)
	y		ġ
	k		t
	s		'(e)
	l		'(u)
	m		s

The Ahiram Epitaph was found at Byblos
and dates back to about 1000 B.C. The epitaph
appeared on the tomb of Ahiram (Akhiram) who
was the Phoenician king of Byblos. The inscription
contained a fully developed alphabet suggesting
that the alphabet had been in use for some time.

g k l   r

m   ' b   š   h

ḥ   '   w   n

t   p   ṭ   s

j

The Mesha Stone was a large memorial stone that
contained a record in ancient Phoenician symbols
about the exploits of Mesha. He was a king
of Moab, around 875 B.C., as recorded in the Bible
(II Kings, 3: 4-5), who rebelled against the
king of Israel.

The words on the stone slab, generally
assumed to date from 842 B.C., were separated by
dots; the sentences were separated by vertical
lines. The writing ran from right to left in the
Phoenician style.

Found in 1868, it was thought to be the earliest
inscription in alphabetic writing until the
Ahiram Epitaph was discovered.

The guidelines, provided by the discoveries of
inscriptions made between 2000-800 B.C., showed

that the Phoenician alphabet developed from the earlier scripts of the Canaanites, the northwest Semitic peoples made up of Moabites, Hebrews, Phoenicians, and others. The system of writing that provided the basis on which the Canaanites built is unknown.

A Babylonian origin is plausible to some. Babylonian was the official diplomatic language of the ancient world, and their cuneiform script was used for the official correspondence of rulers in Phoenicia, Egypt, and other places. Also, the presence of cuneiform marks in the Ugarit alphabet suggested the influence which the Babylonian civilization had upon the Phoenicians of ancient Ugarit. And, the influences of other nations upon the Semitic Phoenicians were present.

Another ancient culture that might have influenced the Phoenicians was the Egyptian. Egypt's political and cultural influence was dominant in the Phoenician coastal area from about 2000-1200 B.C., while the Semitic alphabet was being developed.

The writing techniques of others hadn't gone beyond the syllabic. The Egyptians, however, had created something close to an alphabetic system for their own language and a reasonably simple way to write foreign words. That is, they used signs which indicated one sound. In addition, they found ways of expressing vowels. With 24 signs they could have had an alphabet, but they never used it for their own language.

As mentioned earlier, the Egyptians used 24 letters to indicate single consonants, and some of these letters had been developed by acrophony. To indicate a sound, they used a picture or name of something that began with the sound they wanted. In principle, to get a p sound, for example, they could have shown a picture of a "printer."

In this way, the Egyptians used some of their hieroglyphs to indicate initial sounds. So the hieroglyphs became letter sounds. Deret (the Egyptian word for hand) became the letter d.

It would seem that once the Phoenicians learned the advantages to be derived from acrophony, they could take over the hieroglyphs as well as the acrophonic principle. But, of course, the Semites and the Egyptians didn't have the same names for similar objects.

The Semites were familiar with Egyptian script mainly in the cursive form, called hieratic. Since they didn't know what objects the hieratic signs actually depicted, it has been assumed they gave names to the signs after the objects they recognized in them. For example, the Egyptian hieroglyph (deret), that was used to indicate the consonant d, looked like in the hieratic form. It could have reminded the Semites of a doorleaf (the part that slides or is hinged, as in folding doors), so they called it daleth (door) and used it to indicate d. [10]

Using the principle of acrophony, the Semites could have related each letter with an object that had the sound of that letter at the beginning of its name. Some of the objects could have been derived from hieroglyphs, but mainly the objects would have come from the hieratic, its simplified form.

On the basis of this comparison about how Semitic letters came into being, it seems that the ancient Egyptian system of writing could have influenced the development of the Semitic alphabet.

Of course, it isn't known definitely where the development of the alphabet was made, but some scholars think that it was on the Sinai Peninsula. The system of writing which the Semites in Sinai developed contained 22 consonantal signs.

The Semitic alphabet divided into two branches not long after its "invention." A southern branch was used by the Arabs, and a North Semitic variation, the ancestor of our alphabet, presumably, was used by the Hebrews and Phoenicians.

II ALPHABETIC WRITING

HELLENIC

The Phoenician alphabet, which we, for convenience, will call it, was the basis of several alphabets, including Hellenic, the source of the alphabets of Europe. It appears that the Greeks were the first to receive the Phoenician alphabet in its westward movement. They added several letters to represent the vowels, to have visual signs for a great variety of audible sounds of their voices. Also, they put some of the guttural sounds and sibilants to new uses, simplified other characters, and eventually changed the Semitic style of writing from right to left by writing from left to right. These and other changes, both in the Greek and its derived alphabets, were made over a long period, of course. The alphabets derived from the Hellenic included Greek and Latin.

GREEK

Greece about 900 B.C. was divided into a number of city-states. Because of the physical and political disunion, perhaps, many local alphabets existed before the rise and intellectual supremacy of Athens. In any event, the federation of states settled into the usage of two alphabets: the Ionian (in which the Corinthian was included) and the Chalcidian. The Ionian alphabet, developed in the colony of that name, deviated more from the Phoenician alphabet than the Chalcidian. The Ionian alphabet became the classic alphabet of Greece. The Chalcidian alphabet became the ancestor to the alphabets of Western Europe.[1]

It is presumed, then, that the Greek alphabet was borrowed from the old Phoenician alphabet. The letterforms of the oldest Greek script were very similar to the Phoenician ones. The order of the letters (and their use as numerical signs) corresponded. Also, the direction of the writing in the oldest Greek inscriptions was from right to left, or alternating, as in the Semitic. The names of most of the letters were similar.[2]

It's uncertain when the Greeks began borrowing the alphabet from the Phoenicians. The time of the adoption of the Phoenician alphabet has been set at about the eleventh, or at latest, the tenth century B.C.

The direction of the earliest Greek writing was from right to left, or alternating, as in the Semitic. Some went from left to right, or on occasion, up and down, as the space dictated. Writing that went in both directions, as a field would be plowed, meant that the letters (except the symmetrical ones) were reversed in one line from the following. The direction of writing from left to right as a prevailing practice was established by 500-600 B.C., and letters such as ⪫ were reversed to ⪪

The names of the Greek letters can be compared with the Phoenician ones. The Greek names of letters are meaningless in Greek; the Semitic ones are words in the Semitic languages.

In Greek, ox was <u>bous</u> rather than 'aleph or <u>alpha</u>; a house was <u>oikia</u>, not <u>beth</u> or <u>beta</u>. So the Greeks took the Phoenician names along with the letters to which they belonged.

Also, it seems that the Greeks borrowed the acrophonic principle from the Phoenicians (who may have borrowed it from the Egyptians). The initial sound of a foreign word, which the Greeks had to repeat, became the sound of the letter that the sign represented. The word <u>beth</u>, which was a meaningless word to the Greeks and which they knew as <u>beta</u>, became the name of the letter B, and so on.[3] All of the 22 Phoenician letter names were presumably easy to pronounce by the Phoenicians. To the Greeks, however, only 11 – the letter names that began with consonant sounds the Greeks were familiar with – were easy for them to pronounce.

PHOENICIAN			EARLY GREEK		
Name	Sign	Sound Value	Name	Sign	Sound Value
beth	𐤁	b	beta	B	b
gimel	𐤂	g	gamma	Γ	g
daleth	△	d	delta	△	d
zajin	I	z	zeta	ζ	dz
kaph	𐤊	k	kappa	K	k
lamedh	L	l	lambda	Γ	l
mem	𐤌	m	mu	W	m
nun	𐤍	n	nu	Ν	n
pe	𐤐	p	pi	Γ	p
resh	𐤓	r	rho	P	r
taw	+	t	tau	T	t

Two letter names, <u>teth</u> and <u>qoph</u>, were somewhat
difficult. The Greeks changed the first name
to <u>theta</u>, which became the <u>th</u> sound. Qoph was
called <u>koppa</u> and later dropped.

| teth | ⊕ | t | theta | ⊕ | th |
| qoph | φ | q | koppa | φ | k |

Of the nine remaining sound values, three were
sounds that were difficult for the Greeks to make:
<u>samekh</u> (a sharp <u>s</u> sound), <u>tsade</u> (<u>ts</u> sound), and
<u>shin</u> (<u>sh</u> sound). None was for the soft <u>s</u> that the

Greeks used a lot. One group of Greeks (Corinthian alphabet) chose tsade and renamed it san; another group took shin and called it sigma. Samekh was renamed xi for the sound we give to x.

PHOENICIAN			EARLY GREEK		
Name	Sign	Sound Value	Name	Sign	Sound Value
samekh	‡	s	xi	‡	x
tsade	↳	ts	san	M	s
shin	W	sh	sigma	Ƨ	s

Four of the six which were left were unpronounce-able. Since the Greeks couldn't pronounce the first sound in each of the four letter names, they just left it off. The second sound was a vowel, which they kept. So, the Greeks got four vowel-sound letters that were consonants in the Phoenician list. 'Aleph became alpha, for the sound value of a. He' became e, which was referred to as epsilon. Kheth became eta (long e). 'Ajin became oe, called omicron (o).

'aleph	✗	'	alpha	A	a
he'	∃	h	epsilon	∃	e
kheth	H	h	eta	⊟	h, e
'ajin	O	'	omicron	O	oe

48

The last two Phoenician letter names became vowels in Greek. Jodh became iota; waw became u or upsilon. The western Greeks could pronounce the w sound, as in waw, as well as the u sound. For the w sound, they used a special symbol called digamma, that was to develop into our F.[4]

PHOENICIAN			EARLY GREEK		
Name	Sign	Sound Value	Name	Sign	Sound Value
jodh	Ƶ	j	iota	⊾	i
waw	Ƴ	w	digamma	ꓶ	u

The early alphabets of Greek letters apparently fitted the needs of the western Greeks more than the needs of the eastern Greek people, because changes were made around 500 B.C. by the eastern group. A few new letters were added, a few old ones were dropped, and the sounds represented by a few letters were changed. The changed list became the classical Greek alphabet.

The o sound was given two forms and names: omicron   O   (short o) and omega   Ω   (long o).

The symbol   H   was for a vowel in the eastern list only. The letterform for pi was changed from   7   to   Γ   ; xi   ╪   didn't look like X, but chi **X** , a new letter, did.

Diagamma and koppa were dropped, and
Φ phi and psi **Y** were added to include
some eastern Greek sounds.

Variances in Greek pronunciation occurred
because of the disunity of the country. They had
the same language but they didn't speak it the same.
There were many dialects and differences in the
shapes and sounds of letters. So the ancient Greek
alphabet developed along different lines. The two
main divisions were the eastern (Ionic) alphabet
and the western (Chalcidian) alphabet.

By 400 B.C. the eastern alphabet was
officially adopted at Athens, and the Ionic, in time
and form, became the common, classical alphabet
of 24 capital letters. The Chalcidian alphabet
became the ancestor to the alphabets of Western
Europe. As I. J. Gelb has pointed out, the development of a full alphabet—one with individual sounds
of language by the use of consonant and vowel
signs—was the last major step in the history
of writing.[5]

C. 250 B.C. ■ Camel hair brushes, for writing Chinese characters,
were invented by Meng T'ien, a scholar.

LATIN

The Latin alphabet, the most important of the Italian alphabets, is believed by many to have been derived from the Chalcidian alphabet of the Greeks. Chalcidian got its name because of its use in Chalcis in Euboea, an island in the Aegean from which several Greek colonies migrated to southern Italy. The introduction by colonists of the Greek alphabet into Italy is thought to have occurred in about the eighth century before Christ.

The various Chalcidian derived alphabets— Umbrian, Oscan, Etruscan, perhaps, and others— have all faded away, except the Latin. The eventual dominance of the Latins brought about the end of every other Italian script except theirs. It became, of course, the alphabet of the western Roman Empire.

The Etruscans, from whom the Romans borrowed their alphabet, appeared on the west coast of Italy before Rome was founded. Their background and origin are unknown, but it is generally felt that the Etruscans migrated from Asia Minor.

Etruscan was written in a form of the familiar alphabet, so there was no difficulty with the pronunciation by scholars. The written Etruscan record—about 9,000 inscriptions have been collected, of which only a few are of any length—can be read, but the meanings of the words can't be determined because the long texts that exist can't be compared with any other language. The inscriptions are mostly short tomb inscriptions containing names only. (Bilingual texts are very short and don't help.) So far then, specialists have been prevented from understanding their grammar and vocabulary.

From archaeologists it has been learned that the Etruscans were settled and civilized by 800 B.C. Scattered remnants suggest that the later Etruscans made considerable use of the masonry arch, which was of great importance in Roman buildings. Their homes grew progressively from a simple rectangular structure with a sloping roof to atrium houses with high square or rectangular central halls around which other rooms were symmetrically arranged.

Their elaborate burial grounds, which seemed linked with Oriental customs, revealed the Etruscans with greater detail. Many of the paintings and painted reliefs which decorated the interiors of the tombs indicated that their society was extravagant and violent. [6]

Etruscan script, fifth century B.C.

Etruscan politics, culture, and art may have developed largely as a consequence of the Greek colonization of southern Italy. Although they halted Greek expansion to the north, they adopted Greek influences, such as city-states, but were never united to form a state.
This lack of political unity eventually made them vulnerable to Roman integration, one by one.

From the Etruscans the Romans took their architecture, laws, military system, the idea of paved roads, and other fundamentals of civilization. In addition, it was from the Etruscans that the Romans got their alphabet.

It is assumed that the Etruscan alphabet came into being at a very early date, and that it and the earliest Greek alphabets may be related but independent adaptations of a West-Semitic (Phoenician) prototype. Supporting this was the discovery of an ivory writing tablet, called the Marsiliana Abecedarium, that contained all the Semitic signs. The tablet contained more letters than the classical Greek alphabet. In particular, it showed both san ⋀ and sigma, ⟨ and ✗ as ksi (chi). Presumably then, the earliest

C. 200 B.C. ■ The art of making paper from fibrous matter was practiced by the Chinese. Paper became available to the rest of the world in the middle Eighth Century.

Etruscan alphabet predated the split between Eastern and Western Greek alphabets. The tablet was contemporary with the earliest Greek inscriptions and older than any Greek colony in Italy.

The sunken part of the small tablet, which was probably the copybook of a child, had a thin coating of wax on which the written letters were traced. The tablet, shown below, was dated about 700 B.C., which indicated that writing was established there before the colonists from Euboea arrived or could have exerted much influence on Etruria or Rome.

Also, neither the Marsiliana nor the earliest Greek alphabets can be reconciled with each other or with a single Greek prototype. It seems, then, that the Etruscan alphabet was the earliest alphabet used in Italy.

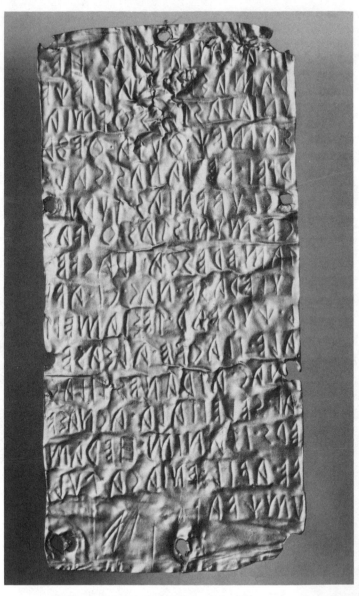

An Etruscan inscription on a sheet of gold
foil; end of the sixth century B.C.
Museo Nazionale Etrusco de Villa Guilia, Rome.

The structure of Etruscan letters was almost identical to the early Greek ones. The direction of the writing always ran from right to left as did most Semitic and early Greek alphabets.

The Etruscan alphabet was modified in time. Their classical alphabet took its final form about 400 B.C., and it contained 20 letters. Sixteen were consonants and four were vowels. However, it was their earlier alphabet that became linked with Rome.

The oldest Latin alphabet contained 21 letters. Inscriptions at the time contained variations of A, D, O, and S. Also, the West-Greek and Etruscan signs for th, kh, and ph sounds were omitted since the Roman language didn't need them. Later on, when the Romans wanted to write a word that contained these sounds, they devised the spellings TH, CH, and PH. This occurred regularly after 100 B.C.

Besides changing characters, the Romans altered the alphabet they borrowed by adding some letters and dropping others. The standard late Roman alphabet had 23 letters.

Three of the early Greek and Etruscan letters may have been converted by the Romans into numerals. Theta, ⊕ for example, changed into another symbol, ☾ and then became ☾ , the initial

letter of centum for 100. Phi Φ changed to
T to (I) into **M** (1000). The kh sign
Y eventually became **L** (50).

The Romans took A, B, E, H, I, K, M, N, O, T, X, and Y with only minor changes.

Sound Value	West-Greek	Etruscan	Latin
a	A	A	A
b	B B	B B	B
e	E F	E	E
h	B H	B H	H
i	S I	I	I
k	K	K K	K
m	M M	M M	M
n	M	M M	N
o	O	O	O
t	T	T t	T
	⊞	⊞ X ⊞	X
y	Y	Y	Y

The Romans used the letter I (the Greek vowel iota) both as a vowel and a consonant. Later, a curved tail was added to I, to create the new letter J. J assumed the consonant sound of i.

Similarly, the Romans used the symbol V (the Greek vowel u̲psilon) as both a vowel and a consonant. The structure of V was altered to produce U, to represent the vowel sound u̲.

Since the symbol V stood for the u̲ sound originally, two V's (double u̲) joined together made W, to take over the old role of V.

The structure of other letterforms was revised to become C (and G), L, S, P, R, D, V, and Z.

Sound Value	West-Greek	Etruscan	Latin
c	˥	˥ ⊃ ⊃	C
l	˥ L	↓	L
s	⟨ ⟩	⟩ ⟨	S
p	˥ ⌐	⌐ ⌐	P
r	⊲ Ρ Ρ	⊲	R
d	△ D	⟨ ⊲	D
u	Υ V	Υ V	V
z	I	I ╪ ╪	Z

C. 190 B.C. ■ The use of parchment, prepared to receive writing on both sides, was attributed to Eumenes II (197-159 B.C.), King of Pergamum, an ancient city of Teuthrania, a district in Mysia. The skins were dressed in such a way as to make them capable of receiving writing on both sides. Older methods probably treated only one side, which was sufficient when a roll was the ordinary book form, and when it wasn't customary to write on the back of the material. The invention of parchment with its two surfaces insured the development of the codex.

Like the Etruscans, the Romans used K only before A, Q only before U, and C (gamma or G in Greek) for k sounds. As a result, we use three letters for the one k sound, as in quoin, key, and capital. Since the Romans didn't have a letter to distinguish g from k, they used the letter C to express the sound of g as well as c. Subsequently, a cross stroke was added to C to create G for the g sound.

Z in the Greek and Etruscan alphabets was abandoned for a time by the Romans. When it was returned to their alphabet, it lost its position – having been replaced by G. So Z was placed at the end.

The last two of the 23 – F and Q – were taken from older characters dropped by the Greeks.

Sound Value	West-Greek	Etruscan	Latin
	ꓶ Ⲗ Ϝ	ꓶ	F
q	Ϙ Ϙ	Ϙ Φ	Q

The Romans kept F (called digamma or double gamma) which the Greeks had dropped for a while. It stood for a v sound, which wasn't needed for Greek pronunciation, but the Romans used it for the sound value f.

Q, as mentioned earlier, was used only before a U that was followed by a vowel. The usage of qu

---

C. 82 ■ Wang Ch'ung, a Chinese philosopher, described the use of bamboo as a writing surface.

as in "quote," rather than just "qote," was started by the Etruscans and Romans, and the practice has remained.

The letters J, U, and W weren't used by the Romans; they were added in the Middle Ages. U and W developed from V, and J was created from the letter I.

The Latin alphabet, which at first was very similar to the Etruscan and Greek alphabets, took its own direction as a vehicle of Roman culture. Its line of development was simpler than the Greek alphabet and was characterized by greater uniformity and constancy–which can be accounted for, perhaps, by the limited extent of its original area of use. Its influence followed naturally through the political supremacy of Rome, in the same way that the Ionian alphabet had become dominant in Greece through the supremacy of Athens.

The history of the Latin alphabet after 100 B.C. consisted not only in the adaptation of that alphabet to other languages but the structural transformation of the individual letters and the development of national scripts.

C. 105 ■ Ts'ai Lun, a Chinese court offical, developed the idea of papermaking from macerated bark of trees, hemp waste, old rags, and fish nets.

lib. XXII. deest folium vn[um]
aut paulo amplius, e libro typis imp[resso]

uelut caeci euadunt armaeque ut uiri super alium ali[um]
tantur pars magna ubi locus fugae deest per prima uad[a]
in aquam progressi quo adcapitibus umeris extare pos[sunt]
mergunt fuere quos inconsultus pauor nando & cum cap[ere]
inpuleritquae ubi immensa ac sine spe erat aut deficien[tibus]
hauriebantur gurgitib; haudne quicquam festinauer[unt]
aegerrime repetebant atqibi abingressis aquam ho[s-]
tibus passim trucidabantur uiri milia ferme primi agm[inis]
aduersos hostis eruptione in nigr[a] e facta ignari omni[um]
se agerentur exlatebris eu[a]sere & cum in tumulo quod[am]
sente clamorem modo ac sonu[m] armorum audientes qu[ae]
pugnae esset neq; scire nec perspicere praecaligine p[ossent]
inclinata adinique re concalescente sole dispulsa neb[ula]
ruit & diem cum liquida iam luce montes campique p[er]-
res stratamque ostendere foede romanam aciem itaq[ue]
pectus procul inmittexur equex sublat[i]s passim signi[s]
tatissimo poterant agmine affse abripuerunt poster[i]
super c&eru extremis fuames d[i]um instaret & fidei dant[i]
bule quicuir omnib; equestribus puis nocte consecutu[s]
arma tradidissent abire cum singulis uestimentis pass[i]
dederunt quae punica religione seruat[a]e fidei ab han[nibale]
atq; in uinculis omnes coniecit ... e nobilis ad tr[a]
pugna atq; inter paucas memorab[il]i populi romani cl[ade]
luc romanorum in acie caesas xm milia spars[a] fug[a]e
& rurum aduersis itineribus urbem p&iere in d[...]
in acie multi postea utrinq; exuul[n]erib; periere m[ulti]

III MANUSCRIPTS IN THE LATIN ALPHABET

Museo di Villa Giulia, Rome.

Manuscripts in the Latin alphabet go back
to the first century A.D. The history of Latin writing
can be divided generally into five periods.
Each can be distinguished by its characteristic
group of handwritings, which were:

> Writing of the Roman period.
> Runes and National handwritings.
> Carolingian minuscules.
> Gothic minuscules.
> Humanistic writing and modern Gothic hands.

During each period, there were many subdivisions.
For example, the writing of the Roman period
was of several kinds, which included capitals
and modifications of them. [1]

WRITING OF THE
ROMAN PERIOD

In the early empire, the Romans used two forms
of letters, capital and cursive. The capitals
were square-shaped or rustic. They were used
for inscriptions and other writing requiring
prominence. The cursive characters were the
originals of our lower-case letters and were used
mainly for correspondence.

MAJUSCULES

In early Latin writing, large letters were called
"majuscules," and there were two kinds.

*The first were capitals, originally cut in stone,
or, to a lesser extent, inscribed on clay and metal.
The shapes of the letters were made by strokes
meeting at angles. Curves were avoided except
where the letters required curves, because straight
lines were more easily cut in stone or metal.*

*The earliest stone cut Roman capitals were without
thick and thin strokes. In the first century A.D. it became
a common practice to cut monumental inscriptions, and
this led to the creation of highly developed letterforms.
Many, apparently, were carefully painted on stone before
cutting. An examination of incised letters cut about 100 A.D.
shows that the strokes in the Roman capitals vary in thickness,
as they continued to do until the early 1800s.
The swelling of the curves occurred about the centers
on the right side and below the centers on the left sides
of the letters. Also, the letters varied in their
individual widths. The variety of the width of the strokes
was caused by the natural handling of a brush, rather
than a chisel, which influenced the shaping of the stone
cut characters.*

PATREM BV
D COGNIT

*It is believed that the disparities in the letters' various
widths relate to their pictorial origin. The earliest*

Museo di Villa Giulia, Rome.

C. 200 ■ The art of woodcut on paper was practiced in China.
It arose out of the use of a wooden stamp to make decorative,
ideographic, and symbolic impressions in clay and wax.

*phonetic signs, which evolved from pictograms by a process
of conventionalization and simplification, retained traces
of pictograms. The spaces that were needed to represent
different objects used in pictograms varied just as the*

DES

*objects varied. The spaces required to present new forms
might easily have varied in the same way.[2]*

**The second kind of written majuscules were
modifications of capitals, called uncials.
In uncials, curves could be easily rendered,
since they were written with a pen.**

*Going back to written capitals, there were two kinds: square
and rustic. Square capitals were used in writing more
important works from the second to the fifth century.
They were generally more formal and closely resembled
the letterforms cut in stone. Right angles were preferred
in the letters. Written square capitals differed mainly
from stone-cut letters in the contrast of the thick-and-thin
strokes—which was greater when written—and in the look
of the serifs created by a pen stroke.*

Serifs were a finishing stroke presumably used to optically strengthen the ends of strokes, usually at the top and bottom of letters. When letters were cut in stone, a chisel was used in such a way that at the end of the line— say the top and bottom of the letter I - the letter was widened and finished, producing a bracketed terminal. (The letters you are reading have serifs which are bracketed.)

Square capitals when finished with a square-tip pen, produced serifs that were wide and square. It was unnatural to make pointed serifs (as they appeared on inscriptions) with this kind of pen point.

SETMA

CRESCEREIAMDO
INGENTISTOLLEN
VERBERALENTAPA
SEDNONYELAMA
QVAMVENIREME
SIVEBOVMSIVEES

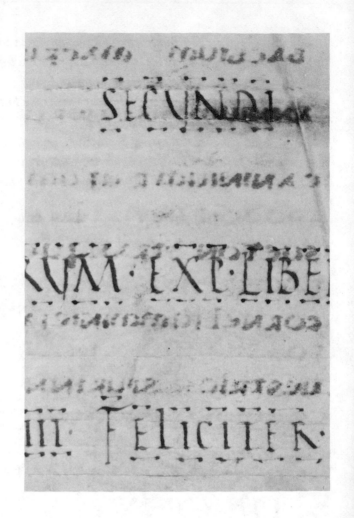

SECUNDI

...KUM·EXT·LIBER

...IIII· FELICITER·

Square capitals weren't easy to write, so their widespread use was limited; a simpler form, requiring fewer lifts of the pen, was preferred.

From about the fourth to seventh centuries, a second kind of capital, called rustic, often appeared. It exemplified the process of simplifying letters by writing, although rustic capitals were used in stone and bronze monuments as well. The letters showed a tendency to be condensed, perhaps to save space when writing on costly vellum. It also appears that rustic capitals were written with the pen point held at a sharper angle than square capitals—at about 60°, rather than 30°, from the base line of the letters. This caused the vertical strokes to be thinner in comparison with the oblique strokes, although the swells of the curved letters continued to occur above and below the horizontal axis of the letter.

ETPRENSOSDOMITAREBOVESET
ADDERENONAFVGAEMELIORCO
MVITAADEOGELIDAMELIVSSEN
AVICVMSOLENOVOTERRASINE
NOCTELEVESMELIVSSTIPVLAEN

CESSIT IN IPSE MIHI DIXERIT CUM CO
SULERET QUANTO SESTERTIUM SESCE
TIES INPLETURUS ESSET INVENISSE SE EX
TA DUPLICAT QUIB PORTENDIAM BIS ET
DUCENTIES HABITURUM ET HABEBIT SI
MODO IN COEPIT ALIEN ATES TAMENTI
QUOD EST IN PROBISSIMUM CENUS FI
LIIS SIS QUORIAM SENTIL IN DICTA ACERIT
UALE

C PLINI · SECUNDI

EPISTULARUM · EXPL · LIBER · II

INC · LIB · III · FELICITER ·

UNCIALS

The second form of majuscule writing, uncials, developed out of written square capitals. Uncial letters were used as the customary book script from the fourth to ninth centuries, although capitals continued to be used for headings, initials, and other contrasts.

Most of the 400 or so surviving manuscripts of this period were religious in context. There were no ligatures (two or more letters joined together) and generally no word spacing. From the

ᴀᴅɪɴᴜɪᴄᴇɴ ᴅɪᴄᴇɴ
ᴜᴏᴅᴇꜱᴛ ʜᴏᴄᴜᴇʀʙ
ᴜɪᴀ ɪɴᴘᴏᴛᴇꜱᴛᴀᴛᴇ ᴇᴛ
ᴋᴍᴘᴇʀᴀᴛ ꜱᴘɪʀɪᴛɪʙ

seventh and eighth centuries on, the use of uncial script began to diminish, although some of the most beautiful manuscripts were rendered then.

Uncials developed from the written square capitals and coincided with the general use of parchment as a writing surface. Their form was caused by the tool (as well as the surface) used to make the letters. In the same sense that it was easier to cut square capitals with right angles in stone, it was easier to render curves with a flat quill pen, rather than a reed, on a paper-like surface. Uncial writing, then, was a round hand, presenting curves in many letter strokes. Because the letters were more simplified and easier to write, uncials were used for the body of books and other manuscripts.

Uncials increased writing speed because the curves reduced the number of pen strokes needed to form the letters. The forms most effected were

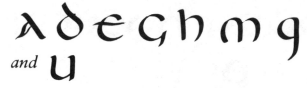

and

Uncial writing signaled the beginning of lower

case letters. In the letter , for example,

the thick stroke (stem) began to curve to the left of the apex; the thin stroke (hairline) and the bar formed a loop. In time, the letter became rounder,

resulting in

BIMUL

TUDOh

NUMINS

ERATA OC

nhilextraordinariu

mplacitetur.nullæq

.translationumsollic

umceteræquetaliæq

ipraeter canonicam

itatii sarcina repen

nihusadscribatur;uc

consciesunt diuinaepr

HALF UNCIALS

As written majuscules developed, there was a
growing tendency for letters to become smaller,
to join together, and to gradually form
ascenders and descenders—producing characters
of unequal height. As a result, majuscules
passed from a two-line to a four-line structure.
Until then, the Roman alphabet was written
between two imaginary horizontal lines,
a capital line and a base line.

      Early in the sixth century, half uncials
(or semiuncials) came into general use, although
examples found in the Roman area date back
to the third century. They were noticeably
different from capitals, and were the beginning
of minuscules—small or lower-case letters.

By now, the upper loop of **B** had

merged with the stem to form **b** ;

δ had become **d** ; **e** changed

to **e** , and so forth. A four-line

structure was implied to accommodate
the use of ascenders and descenders.

So, *in addition to a capital line (which would
become the mean line when lower-case letters
were developed) and a base line, an ascender line
(and capital line—which might not be the same)
and a descender line were established. Ligatured
letters became more common and more varied.*

abern

*Half uncial writing was made up generally
of minuscule letters with an occasional capital
letter, while uncial writing had been composed
largely of capitals, with an occasional minuscule.
The half uncial style of writing, from which the
blackletter or gothic letterform eventually was
derived, reflected a certain national style
by the different peoples who used it. The most important
style of writing to come out of this cursive was the
Irish half uncial. Interesting, no Irish hand was known
on which their letters could have been based, yet seventh
century Irish writing attained a high level of excellence.
It was thought that, some time in the fifth century, a
related book hand was introduced from Gaul by
St. Patrick and other missionaries. Anyway, half uncials
reached a high level of perfection in Ireland
which, in a way, was an isolated country. Because of the
isolation, the Irish scribes with few outside influences
used only this alphabet for a time, and it developed*

rabus illi

em ucnoi

hime·uel

culi carib

into a national hand. In Rome and other parts
of Europe, a number of styles of writing—square
and rustic capitals, variations of uncials and
half uncials—continued and developed side by side
until about the seventh century.

R U N E S

Before Christianity and the Latin alphabet had reached
the Germanic countries, the people there used the runic
alphabet. The question of the origin and development
of this alphabet remains unsettled, but one widely-
accepted theory has linked it to the Greeks, through
the peoples of northern Italy.

The oldest runic alphabet was used
throughout the Germanic territory. It contained
24 symbols in three series of eight, arranged
according to a principle later forgotten.

f u th a r k g w

h n i j e p z s

t b e m l ng o d

The earliest runic inscriptions may date back
to about the fifth century B.C.; the first
certain date, though, was the second century.
The alphabet was widely used; inscriptions
have been found in all Germanic countries
and areas of former Germanic settlement. [3]
So the script was used presumably by all the
Germanic tribes.

Almost all runic writing had been found
on landmarks, weapons, ornaments, monuments

of metal, or on commemorative stones – of which
over 2,500 have been found in Sweden alone.
There were very few manuscripts in which the
runic alphabet appeared. Use of the common
Germanic alphabet ended in about 800.
To the north, however, a Nordic runic alphabet,

composed of sixteen signs, was used extensively
during the Viking era (c.800 – 1050).

In England, runic writing, which over
several centuries had developed into the
Anglo-Saxon runic alphabet of 33 signs,
was used much longer than elsewhere, except
in the Scandinavian countries. The Anglo-Saxons,
to whom the Church of Rome later extended its
influence, used runes for short inscriptions,
such as epitaphs. When the island was converted
to Christianity about 200 years after the Saxon
invasion, the Latin alphabet was introduced.

Runes may have had some effect on certain
symbolic signs, but, generally, they have been regarded
as an invention apart from the development of our alphabet.

Aram autem . genuit aminadab · Aminadab
autem . genuit naasson ; Naasson autem . genu
it salmon · Salmon autem . genuit booz dera
chab ; Booz autem . genuit obed exruth · Obed
autem . genuit iesse ; Iesse autem . genuit da
uid regem ; Dauid autem rex . genuit salomo
nem excea quaefuit uriae ; Salomon autem .
genuit roboam · Roboam autem . genuit abia ;
Abia autem . genuit asa · Asa autem . genuit
iosaphat ; Iosaphat autem . genuit iora · Iora
autem . genuit oziam ; Ozias autem . genuit
ioatham · Ioatham autem . genuit achaz ;
Achaz autem . genuit ezechiam · Ezechias au
tem . genuit manassen ; Manasses autem . genu
it amon · Amon autem . genuit iosiam ; Iosias
autem . genuit iechonia & fratres eius · in trans
migrationem babilonis ; Et post transmigrati
onem babilonis . iechonias genuit salathiel ;
Salathiel autem . genuit zorobabel · Zorobabel
autem . genuit abiud ; Abiud autem . genuit elia
chim · Eliachim autem . genuit azor ; Azor aute .
genuit sadoc · Sadoc autem . genuit achim ; Achim
autem . genuit eliud · Eliud autem . genuit eleazar ;
Eleazar autem . genuit matthan · Matthan
autem . genuit iacob ; Iacob autem . genuit ioseph
uirum mariae . de qua natus e̅. ihs. qui uocatur xps

Different western countries used Roman cursive writing during the existence of the Roman Empire. With its decline, the writings of other nations rose in importance, and a variety of national hands came about. The text hands in use in western Europe from this declining period up to the time of Charlemagne each developed on their own, but later merged into one dominant style, which we now call Gothic.

In Italy there was Curiale, an old Italian manuscript hand, and Beneventan writing, which was better known. Both were derived from later Roman cursive writing and were all minuscule hands.

Curiale was distinguished by careful calligraphic forms. It contained a few completely new letterforms for a, e, t, and q. Beneventan script was cultivated in the writing schools

of Benevento, Monte Cassino, and Salerno,
among others. Many manuscripts of Latin authors
showed this type script. With the decline
of the Middle Ages, it and Curiale were replaced
by the Caroline minuscule. [4]

Another style of writing, called Visigothic, was
essentially the Roman hand that became isolated
and changed into its characteristic Spanish form.
Visigothic became the established text in Spain
during the eighth to twelfth centuries. As shown
below, the tall, condensed letters were placed
close together.

C. 751 ■ Arabian paper manufacturing began. The material was
largely linen. The Arabian and Persian workmen whom they employed
initially used flax, principally because there was an abundant supply.
Later, they used rags from other vegetable fibers that would serve.
Cotton, if used at all, was used very little.

Merovingian writing, early eighth century.

In France, similar styles took on a different development into what was called the Merovingian letter. This French national hand, first evidenced about 625, was originally derived from Roman cursive letters too, but contained, though slowly developed, distinct structural differences.

Merovingian was made up largely of loops and angles in a condensed, irregular style. Though the writing of the seventh century was not very legible, that of the eighth was more easily read.

In the first decade of the ninth century, it was replaced by the Caroline minuscule, except for its use until almost 1100 as a court hand by the rulers of the Holy Roman Empire. One characteristic of the Merovingian hand, as in Visigothic, was an

elongation of the vertical strokes. Also, there

was a degeneration of the basic letterform, as in

the δ (o), ꝗ (t), the letters forming

the different ligatures (aer), and

the use of many ligatures. [5]

Early eighth century manuscript in a Merovingian hand
of semi-barbarous Latin. Gregory of Tours, Historia Francorum.
Bibliotheque Nationale, Paris. Ms. Lat. 17655 fol. 41

commentariũ Adho

historia anglorũ

epistola sci hieronimi

libꝛ doctrine xpiane

sci augustini deepide

sci ambrosii deepide

libꝛ enosi

libꝛ apnonii

lmenci psi euang̃l

libꝛ rufi eppeforor

episcopal

Insular scripts, which were Anglo-Saxon and Irish, developed separately and formed a particular style of writing distinguishable from the Italian, Spanish, and French. Insular scripts were significant not only in the British Isles, but in the further development of letterforms in Europe, primarily through their use in the leading monasteries and cloisters founded by Irish and Anglo-Saxon monks.

When ancient Britain was converted to Christianity during the seventh century, the conversion was brought about largely by Irish monks, so Irish handwriting was introduced there. The relationship of the Anglo-Saxon style to the Irish half uncials and the uncial predominant in Roman books was apparent. The Anglo-Saxon letters were narrower, though, and the tops of some letters

were triangular *and set on stems, or thick strokes, at a different angle. In time, the short pointed script, adapted from the Irish hand, was more freely written and became rounder and clearer in the Anglo-Saxon style.*

nře octis lux tuę
fit. Vt dum ufib
nofcimus:þ hunc

Both Irish half uncials and Anglo-Saxon writing

had two designs for the d $\mathfrak{a}\,\mathfrak{d}$ *and s;* $\int s$

the long s had a thorn that made it look like the

r. $\int$ *The r was difficult to tell from the long*

s and the n.[6] η *Some ligatures were eccentric,*

such as the ati. αt *The Anglo-Saxon*

scribes introduced two runic signs into their
alphabet, for a w after 692, and a th, as in "thorn,"
after 811. Uncial letters appeared as initials and
small capitals; word spacing was more evident.
Insular styles were replaced by the Gothic letter
in the thirteenth century.

90

ctuf apoftuloſi.
paftopalem
dialogopum
commentapiū ad hebpeoſ hum
hiftopia anglofi.
epiftola fci hieronimi.
libgp doctpine xpiane.
fci auguftini defide
fci ambpofi defide
libgp opofi
libgp apnoui
menci fpi euangl
libgp fuif efpefeof
epifcopal
decpeta pontificum
lib auguftini dequantitate anime
lib iumli
officiat
encepidion
lib ppofpepi.
mopalia in iob lib xxii.
fummum bonum
lectionapu duo
gloja
lib aldhelm
lib detpinitate
lib efaiae duo.
catalogui hieronimi pbi deauctopibuf li bpuofi.
gpammatica fci auguftini efci bonifati.
epif fci pauli.

adfutu
fpeculum
omelia fci gregopii maiopaf xxii.
lib ppouepbium
beatitudinif

Library catalog from Wurzburg in Anglo-Saxon minuscule writing (c. 800). Bodleian Library, Oxford. Ms. Laud. Misc. 126, fol. 210r

Detail from an early manuscript of Alcuin's letters, written by Salzburg clergy, 798-99. Oesterreichische Nationalbibliothek, Vienna. Cod. 795 fol. 179

THE CAROLINGIAN PERIOD

*The ninth century in Europe wasn't wholly a time
of darkness. The time was important for the rise
and fall of the Empire founded by Charlemagne.
In the years between the reign of Charles the Great
and that of his grandson, Charles the Bald,
a number of changes occurred which showed a desire
for constructive scholarship. These events greatly
affected the appearance of the printed page as we
know it today.*

*For our purposes, the Carolingian Period
(750-900) was an exception, as was the historical
period following a long train of changes starting
about 1760. Both of these periods—the Carolingian
Period and the late eighteenth / early nineteenth
centuries—fostered revolutions, in a minor key,
in the structure of letterforms.*

*During the end of the eighth century and the entire
ninth century, there were significant cultural advances in
Western Europe. The achievements, called the Carolingian
Renaissance, were inspired and, in part, directed by the
church. Charlemagne and Louis the Pious, who reigned at
the time, took an active part.*

*It was a renaissance because the preceding period had
been a time of barbarism. But a few centers of culture existed
which preserved certain intellectual traditions and made it
possible, with other influences, to rediscover classical antiquity
and re-create art and literature. The process was slow,*

93

however; a long period of preparation by a small group of persons in a few monasteries led up to these achievements.[7]

Scholarly members of the clergy were unhappy with the general ignorance of the ministry and clergy. Similarly, Charlemagne realized the need for greater education and set in motion the literary renaissance, which was to reach its peak under Louis the Pious.

This renaissance was a widespread and guided movement with several definite characteristics. Its inspiration was Christian, and its aim was the expansion of the church. Schooling was, in theory, provided for not just the clergy. It was Latin in character and was concerned with all branches of knowledge.

Charlemagne played an important part in it, mainly through legislation. Because of this, cultural centers other than monasteries were created. Schools were founded. The first efforts were directed at producing more books; scribes were employed to reproduce works of great writers or liturgical books. In the process, a revolution in the art of writing was in progress. But instead of continuing to use a Merovingian script or the writing style introduced by Irish and Anglo-Saxon scribes, a new letterform, the Carolingian minuscule, was gradually appearing. [8]

Caroline minuscules are important not only because they are a permanent manifestation of genius, but because the letters furnished models for lower-case printing types later on. The handwriting had an influence in the geographic areas we now

BEATISSIMO PAPAE DAMASO
HIERONIMUS

Nouum opus me facere cogis ex uetere · ut post exemplaria scrip
turarum toto orbe dispersa · quasi quidam arbiter sedeam
& quia inter se uariant quae sint illa quae cum greca consen ti
ant ueritate decernam · Pius labor · sed periculosa praesump
tio · Iudicare de ceteris Ipsum ab omnibus iudicandum · senis muta
relinquam · & canescentem mundum ad initia retrahere paruu
lorum · Quis enim doctus pariter uel indoctus cum in manus uo
lumen adsumpserit · & a saliua quam semel Inbibit uiderit discre
pare quod lectitat Non statim erumpat Inuocem me falsarium
me clamans esse sacrilegum · quia audeam aliquid In ueteribus
libris addere mutare corrigere · Aduersus quam Inuidiam du
plex causa me consolatur · Quod & tu qui summus sacerdos es
fieri iubes · & uerum non esse quod uariat etiam maledicorum
testimonio conprobatur · Si enim latinis exemplaribus fides est
adhibenda respondeant · quibus tot sunt exemplaria pene quod
codices · si autem ueritas est quaerenda de pluribus · Cur non
ad grecam originem reuertentes · ea quae uel a uitiosis Inter
pretibus male edita uel a presumptoribus Inperitis emendata
peruersius uel a librarius dormitantibus aut addita sunt aut
mutata corrigimus · Neque uero ego de ueteri disputo testamento
Quod a Lxx senioribus Ingrecam linguam uersum tertio gradu
ad nos usque peruenit · Non quaero quid aquila quid sr̄machus
sapiant · Quare theodotion Inter nouos & ueteres medius Incedat ·
sit illa uera Inter praelatio quam apostoli probauerunt · De nouo

call Italy, Spain, and England, and became the dominant handwriting of Western Europe. It superceded all these national hands except that of Ireland. In general, Caroline minuscules eliminated cursive forms to make letters independent of each other and avoided ligatures. If joined together, the combined letters introduced only slight changes in form. Also, the letters were extended. All these tendencies adapted themselves to movable types when the time came to use them.

THE WORK OF THE COPYISTS

The general practice followed in the production of manuscripts in the writing schools of the monasteries in France, which included a convent school at Tours, was to use majuscule letters, either capitals or uncials, for titles and ornamental parts of the book. For the text, scribes used minuscule script. For special passages, a style of writing was reserved which was an adaptation of the half uncial of the fifth and sixth centuries.

   The practice of copying books and collecting new ones to copy increased greatly during the ninth century. Most of the books were sacred books, but others were used to help teach Latin to the new clergy and to revive Latin grammar and literature.

   Manuscripts were copied and illuminated by monks in the scriptorium or writing school of the monastery. The writing tools were quills from swans, geese, and crows; there were knives for sharpening the quills, and different kinds of ink. They used compasses to measure the spaces between lines and a dull, long needle for drawing guidelines— a mark that was reproduced occasionally in early printed books.

They wrote on parchment made from sheep- or goatskins, since papyrus from Egypt was no longer available. Parchment had advantages over papyrus; it resisted dampness, and, if a text wasn't needed anymore, it could be scraped off and the parchment used again.[9]

The illuminators had limited technical and material resources, also, but they were skillful and creative in decorating great numbers of manuscripts— their only original visual art. Many scribes, when they copied texts, left blank spaces or entire pages. The book was then given to an artist who decorated it with illustrations and by adding ornaments to initial letters.

They combined two artistic traditions in their illustrations. The style they used was derived from Early Christian and Byzantine art. They also joined another tradition, the art of the Teutonic and Celtic tribes of pre-Christian Europe. This second style which they integrated, like the art of many primitive peoples, didn't imitate nature. At first, it was abstract and geometric. (This geometrical and non-representational art had

*survived into the Frankish period and was used even
at the time of Charlemagne.) The illuminators
continued the tradition of geometric and abstract
design on ornamental pages. Purely abstract patterns
appeared also in decorated initials.*

THE LITERARY RENAISSANCE

*At the abbey of St. Martin of Tours where many manuscripts
were copied, Alcuin (an Anglo-Saxon who had been educated
at York and who was abbot of St. Martin's from 796 to 804)
guided the creation of many fine illuminated manuscripts.
It was here, sometime before 800, that he also completed
his revision of the Bible. It was a task that Charlemagne
had entrusted to him for the purpose of amending what some
copyists had corrupted.* [10] *A bible executed in Rome in 440,
a copy of which this abbey possessed, is presumed to have
been a model for the illumination of Alcuin's version.
This decorative style was imitated until the middle of the
ninth century. The text itself is believed to have influenced
later versions of the Latin Bible.*

*A preoccupation with biblical texts showed the
essentially clerical character of the Carolingian Renaissance
at the beginning. A primary goal was to bring about an
intellectual regeneration which necessarily would precede
reform of the clergy.*

*Beginning in 780, Charlemagne arranged through
legislation to recruit foreign scholars, particularly from
Italy and England, to set up modest educational foundations.
Consequently, a center for science, art, and literature was*

established at his court. This didn't change the direction of the studies to educate the clergy, but it did have an effect outside the educational sphere. [11]

In order to raise the standards of the entire Frankish Church, Charles issued his "General Admonition" of 789. It directed, among other things, that there be "schools in which the boys read. Correct well the Psalms...chants... works on grammar in each monastery and cathedral church and the Catholic books, because often men wish to address God but do so badly because the works are incorrect. And do not allow your boys to corrupt them through reading or copying: If a Gospel-book psalter or missal has to be copied, let men of mature age do so with every care." He commanded that books that had been corrupted in copying be corrected, that schools be restored in Gaul and founded in Germany, and he wanted his subjects to receive instruction.

Some years later, Alcuin, a close advisor to Charlemagne, drafted for the king some new injunctions on the same matter. He said that instructions should be provided "in the exercise of letters to those who, with God's help are able to learn." [12]

The plan was to teach future generations of the clergy what they needed to know to properly perform their duties, and to copy manuscripts. Also, it would provide another place, other than the royal court, where laymen could acquire some fundamentals in "letters" — but that didn't mean the introduction of elementary education to all. Thirdly, the language was to be clearly distinguished from everyday speech. [13]

The results of Charlemagne's work in organizing education weren't realized largely until the next generation. Nevertheless, some learned men were very influential during Charlemagne's lifetime. They developed a distinct literary production, which had an influence on the people of their time and those who followed.

They took classical writers as their models. In their works can be traced the old Germanic background, the influence of the Scriptures and the leaders of the Church, and lastly, the rediscovery of the values of Roman civilization. [14]

An example of Carolingian literature in the vernacular was Heliand, *written soon after Charles' death. It told the Gospel story as secular epic—a type of presentation that some scholars say Charles' own endeavors encouraged. That is, Charlemagne apparently didn't forget that he and many among him were of Germanic origin.*

Charles' reign was an important time in the history of the Germanic languages: there was a need to write, with some degree of conformity, texts which before then had been passed on orally; and there was a need to create a greater vocabulary to express new ideas. Nevertheless, the European literary and intellectual tradition, even when the greatest writers had already adopted the vernacular, was primarily Latin. So, the significance of Charles' reforms has been judged to be in improved standards of Latin, a more extensive vocabulary, more people who could read and write, and improvements in letterforms and books. The latter was apparent in the number, appearance, and content of the

suuestron tuuem cnoslef cumana· krist endi iacob gode gad
lingos· Thohabda thero gumono thar theneriendo krist nigu
getalde· treuuafte mas· tho het he oc thana tehandon gangar selb
mid them gisidun· simon uuas he hetun; het oc bastholomeus ar
thanaberg uppan faran far them folke adrum· endi philippus mi
im· treuuafte mas· Tho gengun sie tuueliui samad rincos te ther
runu; that the radand sat managoro mundboro the allumu mas
gannie uuid hellie ge thuuing· helpan uuelde formon uuid then
ferne· sohuuem so frummien uuili soliobliea lera· sohe them liudi
thar thurh is giuuit mikil uuisean hogda

Tho umbi thana neriendon krist· nahor gengun sulike gesidos
so he im selbo gecos uualdand undar them uuerode· stodun uui
rigas gumon umbi thana godes sunu· gerno suuido uueros an uuil
leon· uuas im thero uuordo niut thahtun endi thagodun huuat
im thesoro thiodo drohtin· uueldi uualdand selb uuordun cudie
thesum liudiun telobe· Than sat im the landes hirdi geginuuard
far them gumun godes eganbarn uuelda mid is spracun spah
uuord manag lerean thea liudi· huuo sie lof gode anthesum u
roldrike uuirkean scoldiu· Sat im tho endi suuigoda endi sah
an lango· uuas im hold an is hugi helag drohtin· mildianis mode
endi tho ismund antloc uuisde mid uuordun uualdandes
sunu manag marlic thing endi them mannum sagde spa
han uuordun· them the he te theru spracu krist alouualdo
gecoran habda huuilike uuarin allaro irminmanno gode

manuscripts written in Charles' remaining years. [15]

A few examples might provide a view of the literary
aspects and letterforms of the Carolingian renaissance.
At Verona, for instance, there existed a traditon of copying
and annotating manuscripts. As a result, a large group
of manuscripts were produced there for the church library.
About 800, a copy was made of a manuscript, thought to be
from St. Martin's at Tours, which contained works by Alcuin
and others, as an educational and theological manual.
The scribes at Verona had tried earlier to produce a minuscule
from half uncials and cursive letters. The bishop at Verona
had a small group of scribes who wrote a highly developed
minuscule, distinct from earlier letterforms still used at the
court, and a fine script. These scribes made a copy of the
Alcuin book using the type of minuscule which was becoming
the standard one in the Carolingian Empire, and which was
used in a wide variety of books added to the Verona library.

At Salzburg, about forty manuscripts were written
between 785-800 or so. The library there was similar to those
being enlarged in many other centers at the time. There were
texts of the Scriptures, texts for use in worship, as well as
works by religious leaders, including the earliest manuscripts
of a selection of Alcuin's letters. Generally, the Salzburg
scribes wrote either in a round, wide-set minuscule, or a
delicate script—which originated in the north French abbey
of St. Amand. Some scribes, particularly at St. Gall, shortened
the ascenders and descenders and thickened the strokes. The
sources of the texts copied at Salzburg included St. Amand
and St. Martin's library at Tours.

INC SOLILOQVIVM ·

SCI AVGVSTINI · DE TRINITATE ·

Cum me per uigil fidei caste fecisse & exsomne
his me interrogationibus percunctatus & tali studio
scole nře lumga cccccsdi, ludi cacuero lector an utile
sibi hoc sit mihrramgs sinccelccegt nihil subtexchit

prceter Inquit dř nec profcenur ignoscet; Filius dř
apostolur testir est, quid enim ccrt. quosum pctrcer
& quibur xpr secundum ccorne qui est sup omr · dř be
nedictur Insecalca · R quid de spu sco ccurumags
Augustinur dix · ccccgnce mihi breurtter docgidi · qd
dř sit suffregccur · R que illcesit uolo scise quod
& pcccse p cedat · aug g · Probem solum ne quod
pecccccedimittcer · R ubi istad legir · aug g · In
eucegis cum Insufflecurt ihr Insccciem discipulosum
& cit · ccccipite spm scm quora semisereur pcccccccit ye
missce eccpit · & quora secinuersir sccegrecci · R · nihil
fosdaur · ccug g · Alicce multce nercir que quod xpm
ecoccor Inuissccise qd sup xpm uenir Influmine · qd
uiuificcat qd bccpcismu consecccer qd xpm dissegir
qd steplecat orbam · qd chrntccca conccccai · qd nouir cce
pit & segir omnicce · nec solu terrsecethce · scd & ccelsy
                                                    A

*Detail from a theological miscellany written at Verona 800
Bayerische Staatsbibliothek, Munich. Lat. 6407*

The library at St. Martin's in the eighth century contained a miscellaneous collection. Before Alcuin's death, eight scribes there made a copy of Livy's Third Decade

from a fifth century Italian manuscript-an early exhibit of interest in major classical writers. Here again, the text was written in a round minuscule. Also at the time, refined classical capitals were cut at Tours, illustrated by the example below-a verse epitaph of Pope Hadrian I, composed in part by Alcuin.

ECCLESIAS DONIS POPVLOS ET DOGMAT ES CO
IMBVIT ET CVNCTIS PANDIT ADASTRA VIAM
PAVPERIBVS LARGVS NVLLI PIETATE SECVNDVS
ET PRO PLEBE SACRIS PERVIGIL IN PRECIBVS
DOCTRINIS OPIBVS MVRIS ERE XERAT AR CES
VRBS CAPVT ORBIS HONOR INCLYTA ROMA TVAS
MORS CINILNOCIT XP QAE MORE PEREMPTA EST
IANVA SED VITAE MOX MELIORIS ERAT

The use of written capitals for main headings, uncials for subsidiary headings, and a beautiful, round minuscule hand for the text became distinctive characteristics of the St. Martin's scriptorium, and others as well. Subsequently, this form of round minuscule spread to other centers in the empire and was adopted in other countries.

ris bona noluit elicere
et facere cum tempta
tione prouentum. Et in
soldano ipso ato post
a suis interempto pre
dictus rex fuit non sine
dium ut pie creditur
operatione mirabili
liberatus. Tu autem do
mine miserere na

Deo gratias.

Pucelle, Jean. The Hours of Jeanne D'Evreux, Queen of France.
French. XIV century, 1325-1328. The Metropolitan Museum of Art,
The Cloisters Collection, 1954 (54.1.2)

THE GOTHIC MINUSCULE

With widespread use, Carolingian minuscules took on varying national characteristics. Then in the Middle Ages, a second series of national hands, very different from each other, developed from the reformed hand. This second national style began in the twelfth century. The manuscripts of the northern countries of western Europe could now be distinguished from those of the south. The book hands of England, France, and the Low Countries showed a common characteristic of style, especially at first; those of Italy, southern France, and Spain were of a type created by Italian scribes. The German script, which was a part of the northern group, held a place by itself.

The result of this second national development was the Gothic, or blackletter, minuscule of the Middle Ages. The letters were characterized by "breaking," which meant that most of the curves became angular; each letter was formed by a combination of strokes. Beside their pointed shape, the letters had heavy strokes in combination with

---

c.1150 ■ *The manufacture of paper in Europe was established by the Moors in Spain, principally in Xativa, Valencia, and Toledo. With the fall of Moorish power, the manufacture passed into the hands of the Christians. In Italy, papermaking was founded probably as a result of the occupation of Sicily by Arabians. The paper made in Italy and in Spain, was of oriental quality, distinguished by its stoutness, glossy surface, and absence of watermarks.*

fine hairlines to join the letters, and decorative
feet and heads. Also, the style was distinguished by
letters that were taller than they were wide—
narrow set letters, close to each other.

   The Gothic style of writing developed slowly.
But by the thirteenth century, gothic minuscules
had changed noticeably. The letters became more
condensed, adjoining letters often became ligatures,

a quę mœriorę domũ
uabant· a pauimento
̉ dicuntur ędificata·

and the ends of vertical strokes were pointed
(Pointed Script).

   By the fourteenth century, gothic letters
were more angular (double breaking); square feet
and heads had developed. The ascenders and
descenders looked shorter, and many words were
abbreviated (Gothic Text).

C. 1276 ■ Papermaking mills were set up in Fabriano
in the Marquisate of Ancona. It was apparently the first place
to become a center of papermaking in Italy.

108

laxari exilus. ar de metall
folui monachos uber
tamic ab hoftib: circuiten
in predio quo ex bello trep
confugerat: impietans fue

In the fifteenth century, the humanists returned
to Carolingian writing, and it was they who gave
the name "Gothic," meant as a derisive term,
to pointed writing. In the different styles of
gothic writing (including letterforms that developed
after Gothic Text—Rotunda, Bastarda, and others)
were the models of blackletter printing types,
although by this time, the minuscule letters
degenerated somewhat into a less legible and
more ornate form.

C. 1300 ■ The earliest printing in Europe from wood blocks,
of pictorial designs, was done on textiles. The most primitive cuts
on paper, such as "Christ before Herod" in the British Museum, was
probably made about 1400, a quarter of a century before the earliest
line engravings. (In line engravings, the designs were engraved
on the wood block, leaving the main surface of the block
at its original level. The impression produced the picture
in white line on a black ground.)
1331 ■ The earliest known book illustration cut in wood was
an outline sketch of the Goddess of Mercy. It was a full page
and illustrated a chapter from a Chinese book.

aperto marte bellum nauale committitur;
I NCIPIT. LIBER. QVINTVS. CONTINENS
PRAECEPTA. NAVALIS. BELLI. LEGE FE.
RAECEPTO. MAIESTATIS.
tuae imperator inuicte. ter
restris proelii rationibus abso
lutis. naualis belli residua ut
opinor superest portio. de cuius artibus ideo
pauciora dicenda sunt. quia iam dudum pa
cato mari cum barbaris nationibus agitur

HUMANISTIC WRITING
AND MODERN GOTHIC HANDS

*In the 1400s, there were essentially two schools of writing in
Western Europe: humanistic writing, or handwriting of the
Italian Renaissance, and modern gothic. Humanistic writing
was round and was a revival of the Carolingian minuscule
hand. The gothic or blackletter hand was pointed and was a
survival of the gothic minuscule of the Middle Ages.*

*The humanistic script was a result of the revival of
learning during the Renaissance. The humanist scribes, in
their effort to replace the gothic and half-gothic minuscules*

1423 ■ *A "St. Christopher" woodcut of German origin,
now in the John Rylands Library in Manchester, was rendered.*

with older, less harsh letters, revived Carolingian writing to reproduce works of antiquity. This seemed natural, for although 300 years had passed since the use of this style, practically all manuscripts of the classics were written with these letters.

At first, Carolingian writing was copied almost exactly, but later the letters became slightly more compressed and more perfected. The classic capitals were combined with the small letters to create a capital and lower-case alphabet. This occurred in the first decade of the century and later, in part through the efforts of Poggio Bracciolini, a scribe. He wrote roman capitals with minuscules similar to those used by Petrarch. Other Italians contributed to the revival of roman capital letters, though their interests weren't always related to the use of capitals (with minuscules) in books. Rather, some were involved with the use of capitals in architecture or because of a concern for antiquity.

Before this, the capitals and minuscules conflicted; the capitals had an incised-letter look, and the minuscules were pen designs. The scribes realized that the two letterforms didn't mix very well, so they added serifs and finishing strokes to the small letters, to suit them to capitals. These versions, which became the alphabet of the Renaissance, provided the basis for roman printing types.

Printing types, then, related to the written, upright book hands that preceded them. At the time of the invention of movable type, the two styles of writing in general use in Europe inevitably led to two styles of type faces— blackletter and roman.

terrestre certamen .

pro decore et utilita

propter necessitatem

parabat ex tempore

tem sustineret. sempo

N emo enim bello lace

uriam et regno uel

et promptum ad re

cognoscit . Apud m

omanuſ autem popul'

magnitudiniſ tuae. nō

multuſ alicuiuſ claſſē

t ne quando neceſſita

habuit praeparatam .

re aut facere audet in

pulo quem expeditū

endum uindicanduq;

num igitur et rauennā .

An example of a humanist book hand. Vegetius, Institutiones rei militaris,
written at Naples (c. 1450) for Alfonso V, king of Aragon.
Bodleian Library, Oxford. Ms. Canon. Class. Lat. 274, fol. 106v

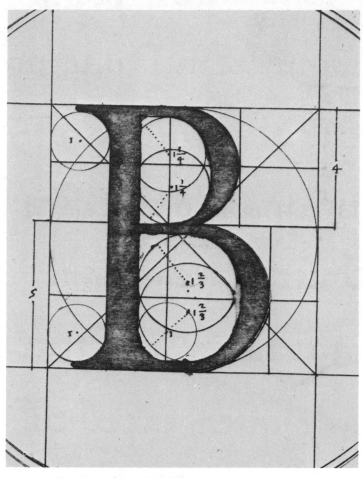

Inscriptional capital by Giovambattista Palatino, c. 1550. Kunstgewerbemuseum, Berlin.

IV PRINTING TYPES

niintiante Pompeio p
pu· defuissent ipse me
sibi numero pronuntia
commendatione Pom
transeundi ad eum om
deditionis conditionib
tes usu atq̃ commertio
sos intra castra iulian
sent admissam inde p
Acie Pharsalica proclai
Deincepsq̃ memī non i

B y the fifteenth century, there was a variety of book hands, cursives, and scripts in use for many purposes— liturgical, legal, literary, commercial, and personal. The four or five leading European hands were broadly classified, as mentioned before, into two styles: blackletter or gothic and roman. Blackletter prevailed everywhere but Italy, where the roman or humanistic hand was confined and its use encouraged by Renaissance scholars.

Printed books at this time were often produced from wooden blocks on which the pictures and text were cut. For others, just the pictures were printed. Apparently, in the latter instance, it was easier to engrave and print the pictures, . but impractical to engrave the text. So printing, in this instance, began as an aid to scribes.

The scribes, in writing the text, simplified written letters, or at least those parts which were difficult for a pen to shape easily.

pore extremo etiam quibus

Types which followed were based on these pen forms and were simplified even more because of technical and mechanical limitations.

With the invention of movable type, the work of the copyist came to an end, and so did the book letters of the scribes.

BLACKLETTER TYPES

The first movable types, invented by Johann Gutenberg (Johannes or Henne Gensfleisch zum Gutenberg, 1397?–1468) of Mainz, were copies of the manuscript hand of fifteenth century Germany. For nearly a hundred years after the invention, blackletter type was the preferred form in Western Europe, except in Italy.

Printing from movable type, made possible by Gutenberg's construction of a practical machine for type founding, ended the books of the copyists. Nevertheless, the earliest books left spaces for initials, marginal decorations and line finishings, which were completed by illuminators so the books would be taken for those of scribes.

Gutenberg's 42-line Bible was printed about 1455 and contained 290 different types, to simulate the current manuscript format. His type and those of the early German

---

C. 1450 ■ Etching was practiced in the Teutonic countries as a means of decorating metal, particularly armour. The earliest engravings— the process of biting lines or areas by means of acid or some other chemical into a metal plate with the view, generally, of its being printed—have been credited to armourers.

printers corresponded, though not exclusively, to the handwritten textura.

Blackletter types that reflect traditional and deliberate differences can be classified into four main groups: 1) textura, 2) rotunda (round gothic), 3) schwabacher (bastarda), and 4) fraktur.

TEXTURA TYPES

Typical textura designs, the earliest and most formal blackletter in type, was used almost exclusively for religious and legal printing. (In a lesser sense, textura minuscules were used in children's lesson books as well, which had been the practice in medieval schools, to teach the script used by the church.) In the lower-case letters, all the rounds, the tops and bottoms of all

runt ibi sculptilia su uiri ei⁹. Et addiderui im ut ascenderent:et

vertical stems were broken. In other words, the letters, which look as though incised letters were models to some extent, were almost completely

BEatus ◆ ā Seruite dño. Euoue

vir ā Seruite dño. Euoue

qui nō abijt in cōsilio i[m]

pioꝛ: ⁊ in via peccatoꝛ [nō]

stetit: et in cathedra pesti

tie nō sedit, Sed in le[ge]

dñi volūtas eius: ⁊ in lege ei⁹ meditabit d[ie]

ac nocte, Et erit tanꝗ lignū qd plantatū

secus decursus aqꝛū: qd fructū suū dabit

tꝑe suo, Et foliū ei⁹ nō defluet: ⁊ oīa que[cūqꝫ]

faciet ꝓsꝑabunt, Non sic impij nō sic: s[ed]

tanꝗ puluis que proicit ventus a facie ter[re]

Ideo nō resurgūt impij in iudicio: neqꝫ p[ccato]

res in cōsilio iustoꝛ, Qm nouit dñs via[m]

stoꝛū: et iter impioꝛ ꝑibit, Gla pri, Oꝫ d[...]

QVare fremuerūt gētes: ⁊ ꝓpli medita[ti]

sūt inania, Astiterūt reges tre et ꝑ[rin]

cipes ꝺuenerūt in vnū: aduisus dñm ⁊ aduisu[s]

xpm ei⁹, Dirūpam⁹ vincla eoꝛ: ⁊ ꝓician[us]

lacking in curves, but present in the capitals. Several different forms of capitals were used,

including Lombardic majuscules,  which

were a development from the uncial.

    In order to subordinate horizontals, the distance between lines (leading) was reduced to the body height (x-height) of the letters, which was large.

Ascenders and descenders were shortened;

strokes finishing on the base line ended in a

diamond shape or pointed feet. The weight

of the thick strokes was from one-fourth to one-

fifth the height of the x-height. Also,

there was a general narrowing of all letters, which added to the vertical effect.

    Textura was the predecessor for schwabacher and fraktur letterforms.

    On the facing page is an example of a textura type face used by Johann Fust and Peter Schoeffer (Mainz, 1459) for their Psalter in Latin (12 x 17). The decorated initials were probably imprinted—one impression for a blue, another for a red.

Rotunda types, a second group of blackletter
types, simply means round. They were, in a sense,
Italian blackletters, closer to the roman tradition
than textura, less massive, and with more legible
capitals.

Sometimes called "half-gothic," the design
was copied from less formal book hands, and
showed the influence exerted by the humanist
scholars. That is, the joints of typical rotunda letters
were rounded, and angles gave place to curves.
The minuscules were more economical in depth, but
not in width, when compared with textura designs.
Other characteristics of rotunda lower-case
letters were: square endings of the uprights;

Artibus ingenijs quefita
Principijs obfta fero m

the **a** was slightly different from previous

designs; and the **d** was changed at times

to an uncial.

An example of the face (with woodcut capitals) is
shown on the facing page. It illustrates fifteenth century
music printing found in liturgical books. The choir book
was printed in Augsburg by Erhard Ratdolt in 1494.

S te leuaui animam

meam deus meus in te confido

non eru bescam neqz irrideant me inimi ci mei

etenim vniuersi qui te expectant non pfundenf ps

Vias tuas dñe demonstra mihi ⁊ semitas tuas

edoce me.   Gloria.   Euouae   Gradale.

Vniuer   si qui te expectant   nõ cõfun

dentur domine   ℣ Vias tuas dñe

sten Büchle
Columen bes
n außzügen/
itragen/ daß
erckmeister zi
ol in eilff teil
en anderthal
s ain posteme

The schwabacher design, the principle German vernacular type, was based on gothic cursive writing. It was often used by printers for their work not devoted to religious or legal literature, for which textura was preferred. Still widely used, schwabacher faces—of which there are many variations—are somewhat lighter, more open, and more legible than textura. The design contains many flourishes in the capitals and lower case.

The letters printed by Chrystoph Froschauer at Zurich in 1567 show typical schwabacher features.

teil in acht teil geteilt / ist
Die überige sechs teil in d

Unlike textura, where the rounds of minuscules

are broken, **rorā m** the rounds of

schwabacher are almond-shaped. **geteilt/d**

The height of the letters is reasonably regular. The capitals relate better to the minuscules than in

textura; some, such as **m p**

and **w** are based on lower-case designs.

125

The fourth group of blackletter faces, fraktur,
was primarily a sixteenth century design.
Fraktur was the result of the baroque influence
on gothic letters and was considered by some to be
a continuation (and perhaps a simplification)
of textura with German Renaissance design changes.

    The type design was based on a letter made
with a broad pen, to which baroque flourishes
and movement, particularly in the capitals,

𝔄 𝔇 𝔗 were introduced.

    A general characteristic of sixteenth century

Deus Jacob miserere mei Et
mitte in adiutoriū meum pro-
prium angelū gloriosissimū:
qui defendat me hodie: et pte-
gat ab oῖbus inimicis meis
Scte Mihael archangele · De-
fende me in plio: vt non pereā

fraktur designs (above), which vary considerably

from fifteenth century frakturs (below), was

minuscules which were half round, half broken.

Particular features included: a closed (with a straight stem); looped and ; tailed and in the form of pegs; and an extended flourish on the foot finial of the .

Incipit Quintus liber eiusdem.
de ciuitate dei.

Ouoniam cõstat oĩm
rerum optandarum
plenitudiné esse felị-
citaté: quę non ẽ dea
sed donũ dei: et ideo
nullũ deũ colendum
esse ab hõibus: ñ q põt eos facere felices.

Vnde si illa dea eẽt: sola colenda merito
diceret. Iam consecter uide am9: qua cã
deus qui põt & illa bona dare quę habere
possunt etiã non boni ac per hoc etiam nõ
felices: romani impiũ tam magnũ tanq̃
diuturnũ esse uoluerit. Quia.n. hoc deo9
flo9 illa quã colebãt multitudo non fecit:
et multa iam diximus: et ubi uisum fuerit
oportunũ esse dicemus. Causa g̃ magnitu-
dinis imperii romani nec fortuita est nec
fatalis: sm eorũ sniam siue opionem q̃ ea
dicũt esse fortuita: quę uel nullas cãs hñt
uel nõ ex aliquo rõnabli ordie uenentes:
et ea fatalia quę preter dei & hõium uo-
lútaté cuiusdã ordis necessitate cõtingũt.
Prorsus diuia puidéia rgna cõstituũt
hũana. Quę si ppterea q̃sq̃ fato tribuit:
quia ipam dei uoluntaté uel prãtem fati
noie appellat: sentéciam teneat: linguam
corrigat. Cur.n. nõ hoc pmũ dicat quod
postea dicturus est: cũ ab illo q̃sq̃ quęsierit
quid dixerit fatii: Iam id hoies quãdo
audiũt usitata loquédi consuetudine: nõ
intelligũt ñ uim posituois siderũ: qualis ẽ
qñ qs nascat siue concipit: qã aliq alienãt
a dei uolútate: aliqui ex illa etiã hęc pen-
dere cõfirmãt. Sed illi q sine dei uolútate
decernere opimãt sidera qd agam9: uel
quid bono9 hĕam9 maloruiue patiamur:
ab auribs ioium repellendi sunt. Non solũ
eo9 q ueram religioné tenẽt: sj qui deo9
qualiũcunq licet flo9 uolũt esse cultores.
Hęc eni opio qd agit aliud nisi ut nullus
oĩno colat aut rogetur ds? Contra quos

contra eos qui pro defensione eo9 quos
deos putant xanç religiõi aduersantur.
Illi uero q positioni stellarũ quodãmodo
decernentiũ qualis q̃sq̃ sit: et qd pueniat
bõi quidue mali accidat ex dei uolútate
suspendunt: si easdem stellas putant bĕre
hãc prãtem traditam sibi a summa illius
prãte ut uolentes ista decernant: magnã
celo faciũt iniuriã: i cui9 uelut clarissimo
senatu ac splendidissima curia opimãtur
scelera facienda decerni: qualia si aliqua
terrena ciuitas decreuisset: gener hũano
decernẽte fuerat euertẽda. Quale deinde
iudiciũ de hoim factis deo relinqt? qbus
cęlestis necessitas adhibet: cũ dñs ille sit
et siderũ & hoim? Aut si nõ dicũt stellas
accepta qde3 prãte a summo deo arbitrio
suo ista decernere: sj in talibs necessitanb9
in gerendis illius oĩo iussa cõplere: ita ne
de ipo sentiendum est: qd indignissimum
uisum est de stellarum uolútate sentire?
Quod si dicũt stellę significare poti9 ista
q̃ facere: ut q̃ locutio quedã sit illa positio
pdicens futura nõ ages: nõ.n. mediociter
docto9 hõim fuit ista sentecia. nõ q dem
ita solẽt loqui mathematica: ut uerbi grã
dicant: Mars ita positus homicidã signi-
ficat sj homicidam nõ facit. Verũtamẽ ut
cõcedam9 nõ eos ut debẽt loqui: et a phis
acciper oportere sermois regulam: ad ea
prenũcianda quę i siderũ positiõe reptre
se putant: qd sit de quo nihil unq̃ dicere
potuerũt: cur i uita gemino9: in actiõibs
et in euentis: in professionibus: artibus:
honoribus: ceterisq̃ rebs ad hũanã uitã
ptinẽtibus: atq̃ in ipa morte sit plerunq̃
tanta diuersitas: ut similiores eis sint q̃ tu
ad hęc actinet multi extranei: q̃ ipi inter
se gemini p exiguo temporis interuallo
in nascédo separati: in cõceptu aũt p unũ
concubitu uno etiã momento seminati.

Cicero dicit Ipocratem Ca. scdm.
nobilissimũ medicũ scriptũ religsse:

OLD STYLE: VENETIAN

During the 1400s, the Italian humanist scholars
used the ninth century Carolingian minuscule—
the forebear of roman lowercase letters—
as a model for a book hand in recopying old
manuscripts. This tradition in writing was so deeply
rooted that the blackletter hand to the north
was not preferred. So, the early printers in Italy
adapted the roman style within fifteen years after
the invention of movable type.

Printing with a roman type face was
introduced in Italy in 1464 by Conrad Sweynheim
(d. 1477) and Arnold Pannartz (d. 1476), who set up
a printing office in the Benedictine monastery
at Subiaco near Rome. Perhaps because they had
learned their craft in Germany and weren't skilled
in cutting roman letters, the first book they
printed contained characters which were neither
blackletter nor roman, but were blackletter in color
but nearly roman in form. The Subiaco letter,

are.Sibillas plurimi et maximi

although it showed the mannerisms of the Gothic
blackletter, marked the beginning of the roman

1460 ■ Woodcut illustrations became more popular in Germany
and the Netherlands. Towards the end of the century in Italy,
many of the most beautiful illustrated books were produced
in Florence and Venice.

type form and was, in a sense, the prototype
from which other roman types descended.

In 1467 they moved their press to Rome
and used a different type, lighter in color and
a farther step in the direction of the roman

& uiuendi genera bóeſti
ualent exerceri. Nam &

as we know it now. When printing began in Paris
in 1470, the type was based on the second design
created by Sweynheim and Pannartz in Rome
and became known as "roman."

Other printers migrated south to set up
shops in Venice, where two years later the type
design of John and Wendelin da Spira (von Speyer)
was introduced. The letter was a well designed
humanist roman that won wide acceptance.

caelo eſſe non poſſunt. Prim
tque fructuoſa: quae paradiſ
ndú eſt:uel propter cbriſti co
nctorum ·qualia in reſurrectic
ıdera ıpá terrena. Si enim ar

1468 ■ Berhold Ruppel was credited with introducing printing into Switzerland.

Simili modo ne conuoluoius fiat in uinea amurcę congios duos decoqui in
tudine mellis rursusǫ cubitū in his tertia parte & sulphuris quarta subdi usǫ
exardescat. Sub tecto hoc uites circa capita ac sub brachiis ungui ita non fore c
uolū. Quidam contenti sunt fimo huius mixturę suffire uineas flatu continu
duo pleriǫ non minus auxilii & alimēti arbitrantur in urina quam Cato abd
amurca modo pari aquę portione quoniā per se noceat. Aliqui uolucre appell
pręrodēs pubescētes uuas quod ne accidat fales cū sint exacutę fibrina pelle d
atǫ ita putant aut sanguine ursino lini uolūt post putatione easdē. Sunt arbo
pestes & formicę has abigunt rubrica ac pice liquida perūctis caudicibus: nec
pisce suspenso iuxta in unū locum congregant: aut lupino trito cum oleo radi
niunt Multi & has & talpas amurca necant. Contraǫ erucas & mala ne putre
lacerti uiridis felle cacumina tāgi iubēt. Priuatim autē contra erucas ambiri ari
singulas a muliere icitati mensis nudis pedibus recincta. Itē ne quod animal
malefico decerpat frondē fimo boum diluto aspargi folia quotiés imber inter
quoniam obluitur ita uirus medicaminis. Mira quędā excogitante solertia bu
quippe cum auerti grandines carmine credāt pleriǫ cuius uerba inserere nō ǫ
serio ausim: ǭǭ a Catone prodita contra luxata mēbra & unguéda harūdinum
rę. Idē arbores religiosas lucosǫ succidi permisit sacrificio prius facto. Cuius
tione notionéǫ eodē uolumine tradidit.

EQVITVR NATVRA FRVGVM OR
rumǫ ac floⱬ quęǫ alia pręter arbores aut frutic
nigna tellure pręueniunt uel per se tantum herba
immēsa contēplatione si quis existimet uarietate
rum flores odores coloresǫ & succos ac uires eaⱬ
salutis ac uoluptatis hoinum gratia gignit. Qua
primum omniú patrocinari terrę & adesse cuncta
renti iuuat: ǭǭ inter initia operis defensę: quonia
ipsa materia intus accedit ad reputationem eiusdē
tis & noxiam nostris eam criminibus urgemus n
que culpam illi iputamus genuit uenena & quis
illa pręter hominé. Cauere ac refugere alitibus serisǫ satis est: atǫ cū arbore ex
liniuntque cornua elephanti & duri saxo rinocerontes & apri détium sicas: se
ad nocendum preparare se animalia quod tamé coⱬ excepto homine tęla sua
suis tingit nos & sagittas cingimus & ferro ipsi nocentius aliquid damus. N
flumina inficimus & reⱬ naturę elemēta. Ipsum quoque quo uiuitur acrem i
nitiem uertimus. Necue est ut putemus ignorari ea ab animalibus quę prępa
rint contra serpétium dimicationes quę post pręlium ad medendū excogitaré
cauimus. Nec ab ullo pręter hominé ueneno puǥ natur alieno. Fateamur erg

The da Spira letters were surpassed
by a Frenchman, Nicholas Jenson (c. 1420-1480),
who settled there in 1468. An engraver at one
of the French mints, he was sent to Mainz in 1458
by Charles VII to learn the new art of printing.

quidem ante diluuium fuerunt:p
altissimi dei sacerdos iustitiæ ac p
bræorū appellatus est:apud quos
ulla mentio erat . Quare nec iuda
gentiles:quoniam non ut gentes
hebræos proprie noïamus aut ab
transitiuos significat.Soli qppe a
nõ scripta ad cognitionẽ ueri dei
ad rectam uitam pueniſſe scribui
totius generis origo Habraam nu
iustitiā quā non a mosaica lege(ſ
Moyſes nascitur)ſed naturali fui
attestatur.Credidit enim Habraa
Quare multarum quoq; gentium
ipſo benedicẽdas oẽs gentes hoc i
aperte prædictum est:cuius ille iu

diluuium autem alii quorũ unus
tis miraculo rex iuſtus lingua he⁄
circuncifionis nec mofaicæ legis
oſteris eni hoc nomen fuit)neq;
alitatem deorum inducebant fed
ere ut dictũ eſt:aut qa id nomen
ituris naturali rõne & lege īnata
ere:& uoluptate corporis cõtẽpta
im quibus omibus præclarus ille
ādus eſt:cui fcriptura mirabilem
na eīm poſt Habraā generatione
one confecutus fũma cum laude
eo & reputatũ eſt ei in iuſtitiam.
rem diuina oracula futurũ:ac in
ic& ipfum quod iam nos uideũs
x perfectioém

De Evangelica Praeparatione, Eusebius.
Type design of Nicholas Jenson, Venice, 1470.
The Pierpont Morgan Library, New York.

When he returned to France in 1461, the son
of Charles showed little interest in printing,
so Jenson turned to Venice.

Jenson's first type was printed in 1470,
and it made him and Venice famous. The letters

uere.hoc uita alimento conseruatur.Ita & alibi iubet dicens.Memoria
recordaberis domini dei tui qui fecit in te magna & mirabilia.Ingentia
enim profecto sunt siquis diligenter considerat formatio corporis:ali-
menti dispensatio:& ad singula membra mirabilis transitus:ac multo
magis sensuum uis mentis agitatio et summa uelocitas:unde singulæ
quoq; artes iuentæ sunt.Quare monet memoria tenendu omnia quæ
diximus diuina uirtute et fieri et gubernari:loca deide ac tepora oibus
accommodauit:ut semp et ubique dei memoria heamus et incipientes
quicq agere et desinentes:et quom inter agendum sumus constituti:ia
cibi et potus tä mundiciæ q imundiciæ q primitiis:qbus factis postea
utimur ad deum nos conuertit.Præterea per uestitü etiam simile fecit.
qd plura: In ipis quoq; ianuis præcæpta dei scribere iussit:ut continuä
eius heremus memoria:et i manibus ipis circuferre ipä uoluit:ut oste-

were round and bold, the individual forms were
very legible and even in weight and fit in all
combinations. Jenson obviously realized an
important difference between written characters,
where the repeated shape of a particular letter
would vary depending upon what letters preceded
or followed it, and printing type, where every
repeated letter was an exact copy which had to fit
all combinations and maintain a relative position
on the page.

1476 ■ William Caxton moved to Westminster where he set up a press,
having learned the art of printing at Cologne. His first production
was a papal indulgence. He continued printing at Westminster for
fifteen years, producing about 100 volumes. England's first printer,
Caxton wrote and translated into English much of the material
he converted into books. He died in 1491 and his press was continued
by his assistant, Wynkyn de Worde.

know not when

e dawned upon

:h people uttere

ice, what better

1 the big and cc

all their kin, a (

enote, unvaryin{

t was the birth

most momento

Another Venetian printer and pioneer
of type design was Erhard Ratdolt, a German who
worked in Italy before returning to Augsburg
to continue printing. He was considered the equal
of the famous Venetian printers and was credited

with many innovations in early book production.
The first to use decorative title pages, the books
he printed were characterized by elaborate borders
and initials suggestive of the Renaissance style.

Characteristics of Venetian types are:

1) oblique or biased **O** stress; 2) minimal

contrast between the thick **b** and thin

strokes; 3) letters in general are wide and bold

in value, especially with the capitals; **R**

4) Bracketed, heavy, and sometimes slab-like

serifs, often cupped; 5) the bar of the **e**

is slanted; and 6) there are slab serifs
which occasionally extend across the tops

of **A** and **M** .

1480 ■ An unknown painter-engraver who worked in western Germany,
called the "Master of the Hausbuch," produced drawings done
in the dry point technique. (Dry point is usually classed
as a kind of etching, though it is actually a form of engraving.
In dry point, no acid is used on the plate, but the lines are hollowed out
of the copper plate with a sharp-pointed tool– a tapering, pointed
instrument of steel. The raised edge turned out is call the burr.
This, in printing, produces the soft velvety effect peculiar to dry points.)

ITALICS

Italic type was an offspring of the roman letter.
It was derived from the humanistic <u>cursive</u> hand
which had become popular in Italy before the
invention of movable type. When formal hands
were written quickly, the shapes of the letters were
affected, and these changes in structure were
exhibited in the italic type designs which developed.
The major changes in the shapes of letters were:
1) the round letters like o were compressed and
became elliptical; 2) a tendency to tie letters
together, creating ligatures; 3) letter shapes were
simplified; and 4) a tendency to incline toward
the right.

Types in this general style can be classified
into four principal groups:

a) The Aldine Italics.

M artis, et æoliis uicinum

b) The Vicentino group.

Corycius suppliciter preces

c) Italics contemporary of Old Style roman.

uit Mundi, priùs

d) Modernized Italics.

The first italic type was cut in 1500 for Aldus Manutius, to use in producing inexpensive editions of Latin classics. The narrow, closely-fit letters

libeat potius

of the humanistic cursive hand provided a style that enabled Manutius to get more text on a small page (about 3 1/2 x 6 inches for the octavo, pocket editions he printed), which saved paper and, therefore, money. The model for the italic was a manuscript of Petrarch. The punches were cut by a distinguished goldsmith, Francesco Griffo da Bologna (c. 1450-1518).

The type was full of ligatures (over sixty), as was the handwriting which was imitated. Roman capitals, rather than italic capitals, were cut and they ranged much lower than the ascenders;

, Meuia even the dot over the i was

above the capital line.

Although it wasn't the best of italic types, the Aldine italic was admired and copied through-out Europe, and versions were sent to England,

H ic elegos? impune diem consumpserit in
I elephus? aut summi plena iam margine
S criptus, et in tergo nec dum finitus, Ores
N ota magis nulli domus est sua, quam m
M artis, et æoliis uicinum rupibus antru
V ulcani · Quid agant uenti, quas torque
A eacus, unde alius furtiuæ deuehat aur
P elliculæ, quantas iaculetur Monychus
F rontonis platani, conuulsáq; marmora
S emper, et assiduo ruptæ lectore columna
E xpectes eadem a summo, minimóq; poe
E t nos ergo manum ferulæ subduximus,
C onsilium dedimus Syllæ, priuatus ut a
D ormiret · stulta est clementia, cum tot ub

though not at first. It was perhaps twenty years
before italic took hold outside Italy.[1] But it had
an influence on type design, maybe because of the
fame of Manutius and the wide distribution of the
Griffo type design in the small volumes.

The italic of Ludovico Arrighi (also called Vicentino)
was cut in 1523. It was a better design than the Aldine
italic, even though it has been overlooked by many. Much
of the present italic style comes from it, through the
influence it had on French printers and type designers,
including Simon deColines.

Arrighi had been a scribe in the Vatican
chancery; he based his italic on the more formal
style of the writing masters of the 1500s. The face
was cut by Bartolomeo dei Rotelli.

It was a more workable type for printers;
Arrighi avoided almost all ligatures. The font
contained long ascenders and descenders, which in
his early versions had rounded terminals in place
of serifs. The generous ascenders and descenders

*N am quę veſtra homini ſanct
S at lętum faciunt · V os
H is quę poſſidet , vti*

automatically provided for more line spacing,
adding a more formal appearance. The capitals,
larger than Aldus', ranged lower than the ascenders,

P rendi dunque' Signor la bella impresa,
  C he' t'ha serbato il ciel mill'anni, e mille',
  P er la più gloriosa, che' mai fosse';
E certo, al suon de' l'honorate' squille'
  S i moverà l'Europa in tua difesa,
  E farà l'armi insanguinate', e rosse'
D el Turco sangue'; e pria vorrà, che' fosse'
R istin di là, che la vittoria risti.
N on è da dubitar, che' Dio non presti
ω gni favor a quel, che' ti destina.
P armi, che' la ruina
  D'e' Turchi posta sia ne' le' tue' mani,
  E 'l tor la Grecia da le' man d'e' cani :
V eggio ne' la mia mente' il grave' scempio
  D i quelle' genti; e con vittoria grande'
  T ornarsi lieto il mio Signore' in Roma.
V eggio che' fiori ogniun d'intorno spande';
  V eggio le' spoglie' opime' andare' al tempio;
  V eggio a molti di lauro ornar la chioma;
V eggio legarsi in verso ogn'Idioma,
  P er celebrar si gloriosi fatti;
  V eggio narrar sin le' parole', e gliatti,

anchora quasi tutte le altre

nno a formare in questo

tto oblungo et non quadr

fetto □

perche al occhio mio la lii

corsiua ouero Cancellaresc

vuole hauere

del

& non del rotondo: che

ti veneria fatta quá=

which was generally followed to maintain a relative visual depth with the lower case. Arrighi's upper case remained upright, as it usually was in manuscripts, but he designed a different capital—swash capitals—to use with them. Overall, the cursive letters were separately formed, slightly inclined, and narrowly set.

Arrighi designed several versions of italics,

N *ulla uia eſt. tamen ire iu*

I *nuiaque audaci propero ten*

V *os per inacceſſas rupes, et*

S *axa Deæ regite, ac ſecretum*

in addition to being a printer of fine limited editions. Antonio Blado, another outstanding printer in Rome in the 1500s, used some of Arrighi's italics. Presumably, a great number of sixteenth century Italian books were printed in italic types. By 1550, though, the use of italic as a book face began to decline. Italics came to be used for other purposes thereafter.

Virtus, tame
teis in-re quacun
ri post tot discri
:um Orbem rex
uit Mundi, priι
habitabat, &

The Basle italic, called after its place
of development as a cursory script, was
one of the first of the Old Style italics.

Spiritu uocem ſtimulante ſan
Exeris, Chriſti Domini De

The lower-case letters sloped more than
Arrighi's, while the capitals, now inclined,
tilted at differing angles—a characteristic
that remained through the development of
William Caslon's types. Despite this, its use
spread to Germany, France, Italy, and England.
The style was firmly established by Robert Granjon,
primarily, and other French type designers.

Even though italic was originally regarded
as a different type face from roman, there was an
indication that cursive would become a supporting
letter of romans. That is, they were being cut
on the same body as the romans, and some specimen
sheets of the late 1500s showed each example of
roman followed by one of italic on the same body.

Italics in this classification generally
accompany Old Style roman faces; they were
designed, although not at first, as companion letters.

It appears that no attempt was made to mate italic to roman in design until about 1700, when Philippe Grandjean (1666-1714) cut the underline romain du roi, a roman alphabet originally designed on a geometrical basis for the Royal Printing House in France. His was a deliberate attempt to make the second face conform in structure to the roman. For example, he romanized (squared the tops of) the *a* , *n* and *m* ; he made the lower-case slope more regular; the slope of the capitals became more consistent; and the lower leg of the *h* , which before then had normally turned inward, *b* became straight-shanked.

Other efforts to modernize italics followed. The beginning cursive strokes were altered halfway between serifs and pen strokes. Still later, Pierre Simon Fournier's italics showed, beside originality and quality, greater contrast between the stem and

146

hairline; he romanized the serifs of some lower-case letters (they became bracketed); the slope

aſſez ; c'eſt le nombre qui opère : fai-tes-en, ſi vous pouvez, un amas con-ſidérable & qui s'élève en pyramide, & je me charge du reſte. Vous n'a-vez ni connoiſſances, ni eſprit, ni ta-

of the letters was regular; and ligatures were elimi-nated. An example of a modernized italic (which was printed with a roman type) is exhibited in the italic designed by Antonio Espinosa of Spain and printed by Joaquin Ibarra in the text of his Sallust in 1772. The work is distinguished by the easily read, beautiful, clear italic.

do derrotado a los que tenia por su fren bre los Moros, y los acomete por un costa rechaza al instante a Boco. Jugurta, q a los suyos, y no querer soltar de las ma que casi tenia en ellas, se detuvo ; viend nuestros caballos, y que havian muerto estaban : se escabulle solo por medio de resguardandose de sus tiros. Mario enton da la caballeria enemiga, buelve en socor

POLIPHILO QVIVI NARRA, CHE GLI PARVE AN‑
CORA DI DORMIRE, ET ALTRONDE IN SOMNO
RITROVARSE IN VNA CONVALLE, LAQVALE NEL
FINE ERA SERATA DE VNA MIRABILE CLAVSVRA
CVM VNA PORTENTOSA PYRAMIDE, DE ADMI‑
RATIONE DIGNA, ET VNO EXCELSO OBELISCO DE
SOPRA. LAQVALE CVM DILIGENTIA ET PIACERE
SVBTILMENTE LA CONSIDEROE.

A SPAVENTEVOLE SILVA, ET CONSTI‑
pato Nemore euaso, & gli primi altri lochi per el dolce
somno che se haua per le fesse & prosternate mébre dif‑
fuso relicti, me ritrouai di nouo in uno piu delectabile
sito assai piu che el præcedente. Elquale non era de mon
ti horridi, & crepidinose rupe intorniato, ne falcato di
strumosi iugi. Ma compositamente de grate montagniole di non tro‑
po altecia. Siluose di giouani quercioli, di roburi, fraxini & Carpi‑
ni, & di frondosi Esculi, & Ilice, & di teneri Coryli, & di Alni, & di Ti‑
lie, & di Opio, & de infructuosi Oleastri, dispositi secondo laspecto de
gli arboriferi Colli. Et giu al piano erano grate siluule di altri siluatici

Type design by Francesco Griffo for Aldus Manutius.
Hypnerotomachia Poliphili, Francesco Colonna, Venice. 1499.
The Pierpont Morgan Library, New York.

pauciora dicenda f;
cato mari cum barl
parabat ex tempor
tem sustineret semp
cmo enim bello lacu
uuriam ei regno ue
et promptum ad re

Immediately before the 1500's, roman printing types closely resembled the style of the then contemporary humanistic script, just as early italics related to vernacular hand-writing. In the two centuries that followed, new roman letterforms in type, called Old Style, developed which were distinct from Venetian. The break was evident in letters as early as 1495, reproduced in De Aetna, a small quarto

Ittera eft pars mínima uo
cis indiuídua.   Sunt au

of sixty pages by the Renaissance humanist Pietro Bembo. A later version of the type design

o, repudiante el rodicabile erugi
:ute & pace exitiale ueneno. Sum
o,cum moderate ,& repentine

was used in the famous book <u>Poliphili</u>
printed in 1499.

Old Style letters that appeared in these
books maintained an oblique or biased stress

like the Venetians, but the modelling—

the gradation from thick to thin strokes—was
more pronounced; the letters became lighter.
Lower-case letters were generally more narrow.
Capitals often ranged lower than ascenders. The
serifs, though bracketed, weren't slablike. And
in a lesser sense, the bar on the lower-case e
became horizontal—a farther move away
from a calligraphic form.

The letterforms in <u>De Aetna</u> and <u>Poliphili</u>
were designed and cut by Francesco Griffo for
Aldus Manutius, a Venetian scholar and publisher.
(It appears that Griffo cut all the roman and
italic fonts for Manutius.) Manutius was best
known for publishing Greek and Latin classics
which combined scholarly editing with art.
His books were widely distributed throughout
Europe, which meant that Griffo's type designs
(called Aldine by the Italians in honor of Aldus
Manutius) received wide distribution. As a result,
the letterforms had a profound effect on later
Old Style designs, and on French Old Style
faces directly; they became the models.

We know no

there dawne

which peopl

Hence, what

from the big

and all their

to denote, ur

That was the

and most mo

Enlargement of 12 point Bembo digital type face design.

151

In the first years of the sixteenth century,
Italian influence upon typographic design and printing
waned, and the course led next to France. In looking back,
representative fonts of fifteenth century Italian roman
types attained a high level of excellence,
perhaps in part because of the quality of the humanistic
book hands that inspired the type. The finest roman faces
of this period, by Jenson, Griffo, Miscomini, and others,
weren't surpassed in the whole history of typography.

With the end of the Italian Renaissance, the ideas
and culture associated with it extended beyond Italy.
In France the dissemination of humanistic thought
was achieved to some extent by the presses
devoted to producing humanistic and classical
texts, and by a king, Francois I, who supported
these endeavors. Craftsmen at the time included
Claude Garamond (1480-1561), Geoffroy Tory
(1480-1533), Simon de Colines (d.1546), and
three generations of the Estienne family –
all of whom were influenced by roman
types, particularly the Griffo designs,
of Italian printers.

C. 1493–1510 ■ A high level of achievement in the art of black-line
woodcut was reached in Germany, where the art chiefly flourished
during the time of Albrecht Dürer (1471–1528) and his followers.
The first book to contain extensive illustrations by Dürer, who was
living in Basle at the time, was the 1493 edition of Der Ritter
vom Turn by Geoffroy de la Tour-Landry. The book was considered
by some to be the greatest German illustrated book
of the fifteenth century.

In time the types the French created and the books they produced evolved into a new form. It was away from the look of a handwritten manuscript with formal columns of type, hand-decorated in color. Their books were printed in formats with which we are familiar today, in sizes from small vest-pocket editions to massive folios. Their books during the middle years of the century were invariably well done, imparting a look of delicacy rather than the simplicity of Italian Renaissance pages. The type designs, an art that became independent of printing at this time and indicative of growing specialization in the field, were often superb.

French types at first were mostly blackletter but were eventually superseded by roman characters. Contributing to the French transition to roman faces was the popular work of Geoffroy Tory, who, among other skills, was a type designer and calligrapher. Influenced by Italian art and letterforms, he prepared a Book of Hours (1525) which reflected and encouraged a lighter, Renaissance style in French printing, and Champfleury (1529), a comprehensive (and less successful, typographically)

1504 ■ The first etching to which an approximate date can be given was a portrait by Daniel Hopfer. An original artist, he was one of a family of armourers working in Augsburg. Iron, which didn't allow a delicate rendering, was the metal used in the first attempts.

book about language, letterforms, and the structure
of roman capitals.

que nõ droitte, quõ dit corbee en rond   Attique
ou en angle. Que ceft que Rond, Que
Quarre, que Triangle. et cõfequamét
quil fache les figures plus generales
de Geometrie. Car nofdittes lettres At
tiques en font toutes faictes & figurees
comme ie le mõftreray aidãt noftre fei=
gneur. Et afin quon naye caufe digno=
rãce, I en efcripray cy les diffinitiõs de
lune aprcs laultre, & les figureray felõ

In the 1530's, variations on the designs of
Italian romans began with Robert Estienne,

is nafcitur in a
tim arbores ho
ouenit colore ca
s, antidotis effic
e relucens. Sign
Diofcorides au
quadam putrila
m exiftiment. C

who took over the printing
firm of his father Henri, and
Simon de Colines. De Colines
designed several roman and
italic faces. The face he used in
1536 for De Natura Stirpium,
a re-cutting of his 1531 design,
had a slightly narrow set,
although the capitals were
large and wide. De Colines
also used a fine, somewhat
condensed italic type for entire books.

1508 ■ European woodcuts were sometimes combined
with one or more surface plates printed in different colors,
partly superimposed.

ribus conſtat particulis. hoc nihil efficacius eſſe ad glutinanda vel citra cicatri=
cem vulnera,ſibi vulgus perſuaſit. Quod ſi recipimus,mirũ eſt Theophraſtum,
Dioſcoridem,Galenum aut ignoraſſe,aut nihil prodidiſſe:nam Strabo ad capi=
tis tantum dolores commendauit.

10　　　　　**❧ Agalochum.**　　　　　　　　　　　　　*Cap.* XXXVI.

Galochum noſtro orbi tantum nomine cognitum, quum (vt
Dioſcoridi placet)ex Arabia & India lignum aduehatur,thyi=
no ſimile,varium punctis maculoſúmque,guſtu ſpiſſante,cum
quadam amaritudine. cute corióque verius quàm cortice ve=
ſtitur,qui penè verſicolor eſt.Commanducatum aut collutum
decocto, ſuauitatem commendat animæ.Aëtius è Græcis pri=
mus quantum equidem inuenerim,à nonnulla ſimilitudine coloris aloës,vt ar=
bitror,xylaloën appellauit:quem poſteriorum medicorum vulgus nomine te=
nus inſequitur.Officinæ *lignum aloës* vocant. Galenus hoc in ſimplicium cenſu
20　ſilentio prætermiſit.Paulus Aegineta Indicum eſſe lignum teſtatur,thuiæ pro=
ximum,odoratum, quod ſua iucunditate ijs os commendat,quibus anima fœ=
tet:ſingularem in ſuffitionibus gratiam habet.Radix denarij pondere pota me=
detur, quibus lentore putri ſtomachus languet. Solutum eundem firmat ven=
triculum. iocineroſis,dyſentericis,laterum doloribus præſidio eſt.Aëtius arbo=
25　ris eſſe lignum tradit in varijs orientalium oris,ſimul & eorum qui plus ad Au=
ſtrum ſpectant, natum, nullóque ab alijs lignis diſcrimine notatur. Quantum
ad odoris rationem pertinet, non aliàs odoratius futurum, quàm vbi teredini=
bus diu patens computruit : ſiquidem marcore ſibi ſuauiorem adſciſcit odo=
rem. Quare locorum incolæ in fruſta diſſectum ſub terra condunt, & aggere
30　multo obruunt. deinde quum ſufficienti tempore emarcuerit, negotiatoribus
vendunt. Aegyptij & alij delibrant ipſum,corticémq; ligni abijciunt.Huius fa=
ſtigia ſumma quatuor celebrantur,quorum notius eſt Indicum,deinde Sapphi=
cũ ex vrbe Sappho, Speon & Hygron,quod ipſum deinde in quaternas ſpecies
cóciditur,de quibus nunc dicere fuerit operoſum.Arabicæ familiæ authores vo=
35　lunt agalochum baccas ferre purpureas piperis minuti ſimilitudine,quapropter
piperallam cœperũt nominare.Sed lignũ duntaxat in vſu eſt,quod nulli volunt
cariei eſſe obnoxiũ,verum odorem ſpirare non anguſtũ.Quod ex meridie deue=
nit,fragrantius quidé eſſe, ſed tineoſum. Agalochum in myrepſico thymiama=
te idem eſſe putat Aëtius quod taron, quod authore Plinio ex caſiæ & cinnami
40　confinio inuehitur per Nabathæos Troglodytáſq; ijs vicinos.Verùm mágones
officinarũ perſæpe pro agalocho aſpalathum ſubſtituunt manifeſto errore:quũ
agalochum maculis interſtinctũ,ac punctis quibuſdam variatũ ſpectetur:aſpala=
thus verò ſubrubeſcit,ſubtérq; corticé atra quadam rutilat purpura,vnico có=
tentus colore.is ſpinarum vallo cingitur,illud glabrũ potius,nec vllis armatum
　　　　　　　　　　　　　　　　　　　　　　　　　　　　k.ij.

1536 deſign by Simon de Colines for De Natura Stirpium,
Jean Ruel, Paris. The Pierpont Morgan Library, New York.

155

ETVSTATEM nobi-
lissimæ Vicecomitum fami-
liæ qui ambitiosius à præalta
Romanorú Cæsarum origi-
ne, Longobardísq; regibus
deducto stemmate, repete-
re contédunt, fabulosis penè initiis inuoluere viden-
tur. Nos autem recentiora
illustrioráque, vti ab omnibus recepta, sequemur: có-
tentíque erimus insigni memoria Heriprandi & Gal-
uanii nepotis, qui eximia cum laude rei militaris, ci-
uilísque prudentiæ, Mediolani principem locum te-
nuerunt. Incidit Galuanius in id tempus quo Medio-
lanum à Federico AEnobarbo deletú est, vir summa
rerum gestarum gloria, & quod in fatis fuit, insigni
calamitate memorabilis. Captus enim, & ad trium-
phum in Germaniam ductus fuisse traditur: sed non
multo póst carceris catenas fregit, ingentíque animi
virtute non semel cæsis Barbaris, vltus iniurias, patriá
restituit. Fuit hic(vt Annales ferunt)Othonis nepos,
eius qui ab insigni pietate magnitudinéque animi, ca
nente illo pernobili classico excitus, ad sacrú bellum
in Syriam contendit, communicatis scilicet consiliis
atque opibus cú Guliermo Montisferrati regulo, qui
à proceritate corporis, Longa spatha vocabatur. Vo-
luntariorum enim equitum ac peditum delectæ no-
A.iii.

Type design of Robert Estienne, 1532.

The italic suggests influences by both Griffo
and Arrighi designs and might have been cut by
Claude Garamond.

Francisce, iandiu liberalibus auspiciis tuis suscep
fauentibus, nuper ad vmbilicum perduxi: vetere
thorum morem, tuæ nunc serenissimæ maiestati
ea semper literarum dignitas fuit, ea excellentia,
ritas, vt eas sibi nasci, apud se foueri, sibíq dicari
nestum & gloriosum putarent: quanto tu magis
briŭ captus voluptate, qui statim à grauioribus il
perii tui functionibus, & curis respirans, quicquic
dis insignium scriptorum lucubrationibus nauite
recitas, tam culto sermone perornas, vt quæ loqu
a reddas, merum sal, meram sapiĕtiam. Quare c

Robert Estienne introduced a new roman face
in 1532. This also might have been cut by Garamond.
The letterforms appear to be based on the Griffo
designs for Aldus Manutius. In particular,
the capitals A, E, G, L, and M resemble those

1521 ■ In Holland, Lucas van Leyden etched a portrait
of Maximilian, which was probably one of the first examples
of the use of copper for etching. As exhibited in the portrait,
copper permitted the combined use of etching and engraving.

157

illustrioráque,vti ab omnibus recepta,sequemur:cō-
tentique erimus insigni memoria Heriprandi & Gal-
uanii nepotis , qui eximia cum laude rei militaris, ci-
uilísque prudentiæ, Mediolani principem locum te-
nuerunt.Incidit Galuanius in id tempus quo Medio-
lanum à Federico AEnobarbo deletū est, vir summa
rerum gestarum gloria , & quod in fatis fuit, insigni
calamitate memorabilis . Captus enim , & ad trium-
phum in Germaniam ductus fuisse traditur: sed non

from <u>De Aetna</u>. Lower-case letters which can be
compared include a, e, g, h, and r. The serifs on the
ascenders look similarly formed, too.

Garamond might have designed and cut
roman types for de Colines and Estienne; his efforts
in designing roman faces have been difficult to
find out with certainty. It is known, for example,
that he was "tailleur de charactères du roi" in 1541
and that Robert Estienne, who was king's printer,
was his sponsor in cutting Greek fonts. Christopher
Plantin (1514-1589), an Antwerp printer, used some
Garamond romans in larger sizes (<u>Index Characterum</u>

Quisquis est, qui m
constantia polleat, quie

1567). It is believed that Garamond cut Estienne's
roman type in 1532 and some of Estienne's Greek

1539 ■ Printing began in the western hemisphere in Mexico City,
by a printer named Giovanni Paoli. The equipment was sent
at the request of the reigning Archbishop of Seville, Spain.

SPECIMEN

ACTERV

M PROBATIS S

ITE QVIDEM, SEI

AS TAMEN DIFFERENTI

VM, TAM IPSIS LIBRORVM AVTOR

QVAM TYPOGRAPHIS APPRIME VTILE

ET ACCOMMODATVM.

Auditui noftro: & brachi

dit ficut virgultum C O

: Non erat forma ei, neque

Petit Canon de Garamond.

& non erat afpectus, & Non defider

iros vir dolorum, & expertus Infirm

uam, & non putauimus eum. Verè l

, nos Autem reputauimus Eum pl

ILIATVM.   W. H.

Final roman of Claude Garamond, 1592.

159

cannot guess

ind the fact th

pressed by a fe

n to select

nass of ideogr

umber of sigr

ain sounds ?

phabet, one of

phs of the hu

letters in 1544, and perhaps later.

Some early roman faces are known to have been designed by Garamond; others are presumed to be his based on comparisons with his early cuttings, the Plantin exhibit, and his generally accepted final roman shown on a specimen sheet (Canon de Garamond, 1592)from the Egenolf-Bermer Foundry in Frankfurt. (The foundry obtained some of Garamond's punches and matrices indirectly through the executor of Garamond's modest estate. Subsequently, they supplied Garamond type to European and English printers.) Aside from these uncertainties, letterforms in the Garamond style dominated European printing up to the early 1700s.

Garamond type designs used today are based on the Egenolf-Bermer letters or, more often, on a type design by Jean Jannon, a seventeenth-century printer who cut a similar face. Jannon's punches and some matrices, which came into the possession of the Imprimerie Nationale, were used in reviving the design in 1898. The types they produced were mistaken for Garamond's in the revival and extensive duplication that followed.

C. 1553 ■ Giovanni Battista della Porta was credited with the invention of the old camera obscura, originally a darkened room with a tiny hole in the window shutter for viewing natural scenes. The camera obscura was based on a principle described by Alhazen, 1100, Roger Bacon, 1267, and others. Leonardo da Vinci described and illustrated a camera obscura in his notebooks.

Characteristics of widely copied Garamond roman types are: 1) the letters are open and clear;

w s one to eva

2) the capitals are relatively large; 3) there is a slight tilt to the angles of the swells of the round letters; 4) the face has wide concave serifs

which angle out sharply from the stem I and end

in a fairly crisp manner; 5) there are small loops

on the a and e ; 6) the a is narrow; 7) the

serifs on the T slant at different angles;

8) A has a high bar, a pointed apex; 9) r

has a concave serif (unlike the original) with a

teardrop ear; 10) L has a short horizontal stroke;

11) C has a wide opening, a short terminal stroke;

12) g has a rectangular ear that points to the

right; and 13) the M has a vertical hairline

that leans inward.

Garamond died in 1561 with little money, so his wife tried to realize something by the sale of his punches and matrices. Christopher Plantin was in Paris at the time, having been forced to leave Antwerp temporarily because of suspected heresy, and he attended the sale of Garamond's effects.[2] Conceivably, he acquired some of Garamond's stock, because a publication of Plantin's issued in 1567 showed two large sizes of roman which appeared to be the same as Garamond's specimens. That was a year after Plantin founded his press. In the late 1500s it grew to become the largest and, perhaps, the most progressive printing and publishing house in Europe.

His types came from French sources; he had purchased fonts used by Simon de Colones, as well as at the sale of Garamond's material. Robert Granjon, another Frenchman, designed several series for him.

Plantin, who was a Frenchman and whose books reflected it, was an example of the printer who left France for the Netherlands because of restrictions and censorship placed on presses by the Church and the government. French Old Style designs continued until the 1700s, but the greatness of French book production, which existed during the first half of the 1500s, declined.

The center for printing and type founding passed from France to the Netherlands. Publishing firms, such as the House of Elzevir, dominated book markets of Europe at different times from 1583 to 1680. The Dutch continued the French sixteenth century typographic style, although a slight increase in contrast between the thick and thin strokes in the lower case became evident. Later in the 1600s, especially after 1647, the Elzevir types were almost always cut by Christoffel van Dyck. His letters

ardius aliqua

ɔ acta res eſt.

lis, Zelandiſ

n deſignaret

were precisely cut, closely fitted, and flawless.

Characteristics of some Dutch letters were an increase in the x-height of the lower-case letters and a more narrow set, as well as an increase in contrast, the first two of which were practical

---

1611 ■ A Latin treatise by Dominis described the additive system of complementary colors.

e know not wh
ere dawned up
nich people utt
ence, what bett
om the big and
d all their kin,
denote, unvary
hat was the birt
d most momen

Enlargement of 12 point Janson digital type face design.

considerations for the production of commercial printing. These characteristics can be seen in the Janson type cut by Anton Janson (or as some believe, byMiklos Kis, a Hungarian type cutter who worked in Amsterdam).[3]

GHIJKLMN(
abcdefghijklm

An important factor in the distribution of Dutch types, even though Holland was a principal trading nation during the 1600s, was their acceptance in England. At the end of the seventeenth century, it was said there were more Dutch types in England than English, because few persons were trained in punch cutting. The Crown interfered with printing to such an extent that type-founding wasn't free to develop until 1637, when it was officially separated from printing by a decree.

The extensive use of Dutch types in England ended shortly after William Caslon (originally Caslona, after a town in southern Spain from which his father came) established his type foundry in

---

1642 ■ Galileo died. On Christmas Day of the same year in England, Isaac Newton was born. ■ The earliest dated mezzotint, a portrait, was drawn by Ludwig van Siegen.

London. Caslon, an engraver, became interested
in cutting punches for type founders and, because of
his work, was encouraged to enter the type-founding
business. His first specimen sheet in 1734 contained
thirty-eight fonts. Beside roman and italic faces,
the specimen included several fonts of Greek, Hebrew,
and other alphabets. All except three were designed
and cut by Caslon[4] and represented fourteen years of

Quoufque tandem abu
tientia noftra ? quam
ror ifte tuus eludet ? c
fe effrenata jactabit au
nocturnum præfidium
bis vigiliæ, nihil timor
A B C D E F G H I J K

1666 ■ Isaac Newton described light in its color spectrum.
1683 ■ A handbook, Mechanick Exercises, or the Doctrine
of Handy-Works, was published by Joseph Moxon of Yorkshire. It was a
republication of 24 papers about the technical processes of printing.

work. Each letter was precisely cut at the end of a steel punch with few instruments of precision. (It normally took over a day for a skilled punch-cutter to cut one punch.)

The type met with immediate success and ended the dominance of Dutch type founders in supplying English printers with type. Caslon designs have been used ever since, of course.

Caslon's roman and italic were based largely on Dutch types of the late 1600s, but the precision of the cutting and a somewhat vertical emphasis were eighteenth century. The lower-case serif structure, as well as a number of characters, retained the earlier Dutch forms, but the contrast of the stem and hairline strokes was more pronounced.

The widespread use of Caslon type in the American colonies and elsewhere came about largely through the expansion and influence of the British Empire. In the process, England became a center of publishing, with an accompanying typographic industry.

1714 ■ A British patent was granted to Henry Hill for "an Artificial Machine or Method for the Impressing or Transcribing of Letters Singly or Progressively one after another, as in Writing, whereby all Writing whatever may be Engrossed in Paper or Parchment so Neat and Exact as not to be distinguished from Print."
1719 ■ Rene de Reaumur, a French physicist and inventor, recommended the manufacture of paper from wood pulp.
1722 ■ LeBlon, a German living in Paris, used three color printing with red, yellow, and blue plates.

know not w
re dawned u
ich people ut
nce, what bet
m the big and
l all their kin
lenote, unvar
at was the bi
l most mome

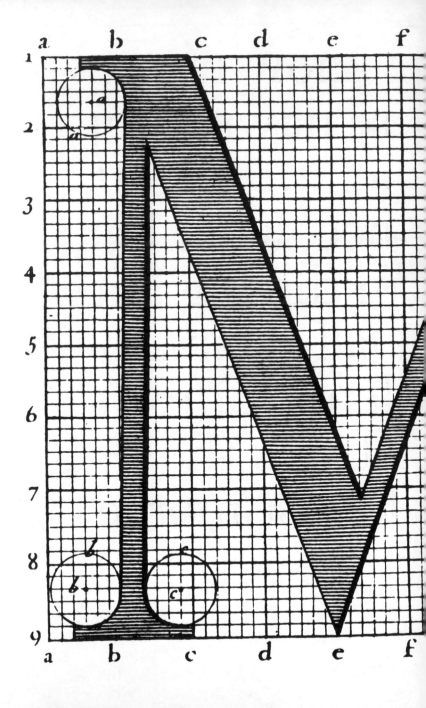

TRANSITIONAL TYPES

A major change from the Old Style designs occurred in 1692, when a new series of types was ordered for the Royal Printing House in France by a commission of the Académie des Sciences. It was recommended that a roman alphabet be designed on a geometrical basis. Each letter design was based on a square, the sides of which were divided into 48 parts. So 2,304 squares comprised each letter square. The purpose of the system was to permit

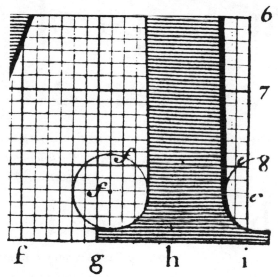

the exact type-cutting of the letters, particularly in the smaller sizes, rather than to dictate or restrict the form the creative letters would take.[5] The punches were cut by Philippe Grandjean, a royal type-cutter. By 1702 the new type, romain du roi, was completed.

The shadings of the type were largely vertical,
and the contrast between the thick and thin strokes
was more noticeable than with Old Style types;

La première

grand spectacle

par sa parole,

C'est par où

the somewhat condensed letters had straight, sharp serifs
with very little bracketing. Some serifs at the top of lower-
case letters extended on both sides of the stem,

as on **b** , **d** , **h** , **i** , *and* **I** .

This French design was considered the forerunner
of Transitional types—designs based on Old Style fonts,
coupled with features of the type style called Modern.

1727 ■ *In an early effort to reproduce pictures, J. H. Schulze*
used a mixture of silver nitrate and chalk under stencilled letters,
to produce a darkening action caused by light.

The form the Grandjean letters took was possible
because type founding, which reached a high
degree of perfection in the 1700s, had heretofore
restricted the making of fine, tapering and
sharp serifs. Also, considerable technical
progress had been made in paper production –
particularly smoother papers – and, perhaps related,
there was widespread interest in copperplate engraving.

The romain du roi strongly influenced French
craftsmen, though they were forbidden from copying the
new face. One of the outstanding punch cutters of the time,
Pierre Simon Fournier (1712-1768) evaded the restriction
by designing a similar face in 1742. He was the last of a
French family who had been in type founding and type design
for several generations. Trained in art, he turned to type and
type ornament design. His letters were slightly different from

répondit froidement le Munition-
naire , on ne pend pas quelqu'un qui
peut difpofer de cent mille écus ;
& là-deffus ils paffèrent dans le ca-
binet. Un inftant après , Monfieur
le Général en fortit perfuadé que
c'étoit un fort honnête-homme.

Ceci nous apprend qu'on ne doit

Collége de Reims

the <u>romain du roi</u> in that he made the proportions
of the letters more narrow, and he added a slight

bracket to the serifs. **VE** *The advantages of*

a narrow set suggested in the Grandjean design
were recognized, and other characteristics of
the Grandjean design as well were followed for Dutch
printing. Particularly influenced was J. M. Fleischman,
who cut twenty new alphabets (1730-1768) for use
in producing pocket books. All the fonts were condensed,
with fine hairlines and thin serifs.[6]

munis ignarus. Quis enim
do bonorum confuetudinem
amico miffas, offenfione
dium protulit, palamque

1739 ■ *Stereotyping (the process of making a duplicate printing plate
from a mold or matrix of composed type) was invented by William Ged,
a goldsmith of Edinburgh. Using plaster of Paris, Ged cast a text page;
the mold was used for producing a plate of a new text page. The process
wasn't adopted by Scottish printers, however, because they felt
it would adversely affect their jobs. Six years later, the concept
was revived by Firmin Didot. His page plates were cast from recessed,
rather than raised, molds.*

MOD
ES CAR
DE L'IMI
r DES AUTRES CHOSES
NOUVELLEM
n-Pierre Fournier le j

Jamque eadem fummis pariter, minimifque libido:
Nec melior pedibus filicem quæ conterit atrum;
Quam quæ longorum vehitur cervice Syrorum.
Ut fpectet ludos, conducit Ogulnia veftem,
Conducit comites, fellam, cervical, amicas,
Nutricem, et flavam, cui det mandata, puellam.
Hæc tamen argenti fupereft quodcumque paterni
Lævibus athletis, ac vafa noviffima donat.
Multis res angufta domi eft: fed nulla pudorem
Paupertatis habet; nec fe metitur ad illum,
Quem dedit hæc pofuitque modum. Tamen utile quid fit,
Profpiciunt aliquando viri; frigufque, famemque,
Formica tandem quidam expavere magiftra.
Prodiga non fentit pereuntem fœmina cenfum:
At velut exhaufta redivivus pullulet arca
Nummus, et e pleno femper tollatur acervo,
Non unquam reputat, quanti fibi gaudia conftent.
Sunt quas eunuchi imbelles, ac mollia femper
Ofcula delectent, et defperatio barbæ,
Et quod abortivo non eft opus. Illa voluptas
Summa tamen, quod jam calida et matura juventa
Inguina traduntur medicis, jam pectine nigro.

K   Ergo

Baskerville's letters for <u>Satyrea</u>, Juvenal and Persius, 1761.
The Pierpont Morgan Library, New York.

JOHN BASKERVILLE

The accepted beginning of Transitional letters
was the work of John Baskerville in England. His
printing and typographic style later affected
the Modern designs of Francois Ambrose Didot
in France, Giambattista Bodoni in Italy, and
Joaquin Ibarra in Spain.

The Baskerville letters showed a greater
refinement, perhaps, than the letters of William
Caslon, with which his designs were compared.
The Baskerville face was round and graceful,
with heavily filleted stems and bracketed serifs.
When set in mass, it gave an effect of lightness
and openness. The roman letters, unlike the italic,
were very wide. His characters were in line with
the tendency toward lighter type faces which
developed in European printing; and although his
fonts never had much success in England, they
had a significant influence on later developments
in English and European typography and printing.[7]

John Baskerville (1706-1775) lived during a time
when the commercial middle classes of England were coming
to power. When he was a young man, Baskerville went to
Birmingham, which had a population of about 30,000 and
was a town noted for its manufacturing. His first job
(although it isn't based on the best authority) was as a
servant for a clergyman. The clergyman, so the story has
been told, found that Baskerville was skilled in penmanship

and had him teach writing to the young people of the parish. Later, when a position as writing-master became available, he took it and taught writing and bookkeeping.

During this time, Baskerville became interested in calligraphy and applied this skill in stonecutting. A specimen of his work that remains—a small (27 x 22 cm.) slate slab—contains the inscription: "Grave Stones Cut in any of the Hands By John Baskervill Writing-Master." (He added the final _e_ to his name later on.)

In the early 1730s, a manufacturer named John Taylor came to Birmingham and introduced japanned ware articles such as gilt buttons and painted snuff boxes. Taylor created a fortune out of the business, so Baskerville decided to produce painted and japanned goods, also. He was a skilled draftsman and could paint, and he learned the business.[8]

Apparently, Baskerville had some artistic sense and business knowledge, and his business prospered. By 1749, his firm was producing a variety of products, including candlesticks, stands, and trays that were reported to be well designed, highly finished, and expensive, although no specimens remain—or at least no recognizable specimens, since none was signed.[9]

In a brief time, Baskerville amassed a fortune in the business. He built an imposing house, expensively furnished, on seven acres which he called Easy Hill, outside Birmingham, and it was there that he established his printing business.

About 1750, a Mrs. Richard Eaves went to live

at Easy Hill, perhaps as a housekeeper. She was married, but her husband had been forced to leave the country because of some fraudulent practice about a relation's will. In any event, she and her children went to live at Baskerville's house. When Mr. Eaves died in 1764, Baskerville married her. They had one son who died in infancy.

When Baskerville began his work in type design and printing, he was about forty-five years old and living comfortably. He spent seven or eight years in creating his type designs and experimenting with ink and paper. The punches for his type were cut by John Handy, and several years passed before a font was completed. The work in preparing his type, as reported by Reed's A History of the Old English Letter Foundries (1887), was described: "He had at first to design his model alphabet letter by letter, so that each letter could bear its true relation to the other letters, on a scale of absolute proportion. The design fixed, the next step was to decide the particular size on which he would begin. Then came the critical manual operation of cutting each letter separately in relief, on steel, to form the punch. Each punch would then have to be hardened and struck into copper to form a matrix, and each matrix would need to be justified and adjusted to the type mold, so as to produce a type not only an exact counterpart of the punch, but absolutely square with each other letter of the font. The molds for casting type would have to be constructed each of a large number of separate pieces of iron and wood, fitted together with the most delicate precision, so that each type would come out uniform in height and body. When matrixes and molds were ready, the operation of casting would ensue. The types would require dressing before they could be used: a delicate operation, consisting in the smoothing away of every chance irregularity left by the casting, without interfering with the mathematical height and squareness of the letter."

Baskerville's first book, the Latin Virgil, came out in 1757, and it was an astonishing book, primarily for its qualities of presswork, inking, type sizes (generally), and line spacing. In 1758, he issued a Milton in two volumes which perhaps was mainly interesting because of the preface he wrote for it. He said that, having been an early admirer of the beauty of letters, he had tried to produce a true alphabet according to what he conceived to be their true proportions. It was not his desire, he continued, to print many books, but books of consequence which the public might purchase at a price that would repay the care and expense he had spent on them. His Milton was followed by fifty-four other books ranging from a folio Bible in 1763 (when Baskerville was printer to Cambridge University) to Charles Bowlker's The Art of Angling in 1774.

In printing a book, Baskerville, soon after his Virgil was issued, began a practice of pressing the dampened sheets from the press, probably between heated plates of copper. It dried the sheet, set the ink, and gave the surface a glossy finish—something no other printer had done.

Baskerville's other contribution to papermaking was the use of wove paper, which he was the first to use, in the Latin Virgil. Wove paper—in which the marks of the wires in the mesh of the paper-maker's mold weren't seen in the finished paper—added variety and, maybe, interest to the look of a book. And it gave the printer a choice in selecting paper with type, ink, and illustration. Also,

PUBLII VIRGILII

MARONIS

BUCOLICA,

GEORGICA,

ET

AENEIS.

BIRMINGHAMIAE:
Typis JOHANNIS BASKERVILLE.
MDCCLVII.

it made possible the better use of type faces with hairlines.

It isn't known to what extent Baskerville was responsible for the production of the first wove paper in England and Europe. It appears that it wasn't an invention of his, although some writers on the subject refer to his papermaking. There is no evidence that Baskerville ever owned the equipment used in making paper. Several times in his correspondence, he mentioned buying paper, and research suggests that the credit should go to James Whatman (1702-1759).[10] At any rate, Baskerville was the first to direct making wove paper in Europe, which was slow in finding its way into the hands of printers.

Baskerville used many different kinds of paper at his press, some of which came from Whatman's mill. In all, Baskerville used wove paper in only a few of his books. Normally, he used laid papers which varied in weight and texture, though he preferred light papers for his better work. The sheets of most of his finer books were pressed after printing, except when he printed for others. It seems they didn't prefer it.

Baskerville's character and his work were severely criticized by other printers in his time. They were particularly harsh about his type design, setting, and his smooth paper, and in spite of his artistic success, he failed to make printing a paying venture. Fortunately, he retained the japanning business.

Twenty-seven of Baskerville's books were printed either for other publishers or for the authors. So there was some demand for his work, even though there was prejudice that his prices were high. In fact, his books cost little more than did the average one of his day. The books he printed for himself were expensive.

Then there's the story that Benjamin Franklin, in a letter to Baskerville, told him of a practical joke Franklin played on a critic of Baskerville's types. The critic said that Baskerville's types would be "the means of blinding all the readers in the nation owing to the thin and narrow strokes of the letters." Franklin gave the critic a specimen of Caslon's types with Caslon's name removed, said it was Baskerville's, and asked for a specific criticism. The critic, an author whose book was printed in the same Caslon face, responded at great length about faults he felt were very apparent in the type. Before he had finished, he complained that his eyes were suffering from the strain of reading the text.

All of Baskerville's printing was done in sixteen years. He printed about sixty-six or sixty-seven books. Some were reprints of his earlier works, so he really produced about fifty to sixty original books. They weren't of equal merit, of course, and his reputation rests upon a few.

One of the best was the Latin Juvenal and Persius, printed in 1761. It was very simply arranged. The argument to each satire was set in a large italic, and the text was a more leaded roman than his Virgil. Running heads were set in spaced italic capitals. The imposition was formal, the margins carefully regarded, and the type was clear.

A recurring shortcoming of his work was corrections

e know not

ere dawned

nich people

ence, what b

om the big a

d all their ki

denote, unv

hat was the k

d most mon

Enlargement of 12 point Baskerville L.D. digital type face design.
Mergenthaler Linotype Stempel Haas.

1772 ■ *Wilhelm Haas, a type founder at Basle, built a printing press*
with a framework of cast iron and with an iron platen.
Its development was delayed, however.

and cancellations. When mistakes were discovered in the printed sheets, he used cancellations. Almost half of his books have obvious cancels, some of which were extensive. Also, many errors were undetected by him. [11]

Toward the end of his life, Baskerville used type which was worn and broken, especially in a few classics he printed between 1772-1774. Before then, it seems it was his custom to melt the types when one book was completed, so that he always printed with new faces. [12]

Baskerville continued in printing and publishing though his books weren't profitable. By this time, he had grown "heartily tired of and repent I every attempted" printing. And, "the Book-sellers did not choose to encourage" him. After 1765, little appeared from his press, and several times during those later years, he tried to sell his types— to the Academie des Sciences at Paris, to the court of Russia, to Denmark, to the English government—without success. In a letter to Benjamin Franklin, then in Paris on a diplomatic mission, Baskerville asked him to aid in the sale to the Imprimerie Royale. He said that another of the reasons for wanting to sell his type was "the death of my son and intended successor." Franklin replied that the condition of France at the time was such that it prevented them from making a purchase of that kind.

For a time, he placed his printing office in the hands of his foreman. Later, he resumed control and continued to print until his death.

Baskerville's printing was a financial failure for several reasons. For one thing, he did something new.

He produced type different from what was available, and the printers whose shops were stocked with Caslon and Dutch types didn't think it was as good. So, they didn't replace type which could be used for books that were good enough to be sold. In the second place, none of Baskerville's books was inexpensive. And most of his books were reprints. [13]

Many books today are printed with types which are copies of Caslon, Baskerville, or Bodoni faces, or designs influenced by these types. The influences of the eighteenth century book – the types, settings, page layout, ink, and paper – have been lasting. However, there was a time, until recently, when the works of Baskerville and Bodoni were generally denounced.

The history of the developments that made a new thing of the eighteenth century printed page is primarily the history of changing type forms and of changing ways of setting type. This change in type forms progressed along two lines. The first was the creation of a letterform characterized by increased differences in the width of the thick and thin strokes, by a vertical emphasis to the letters and the finishing of the letters with a thin hairline serif – bracketed at first; then slightly bracketed; then a hairline devoid of brackets. The other major tendency, which generally preceded this, was the effort to perfect existing Old Style letterforms, as seen in the types of William Caslon.

Although the connection among the characteristic styles of Caslon, Baskerville and Bodoni isn't easily seen, there was a connection provided by what is sometimes called the spirit of the time. Baskerville moved in the direction *of the Modern face and the desire for fine printing with order, clarity, and simplicity.*

us? an Meliboei?

me quum fæpe roꬶ

ːm dignus amari)

ære, Menalca.

ꞌ *E X T A.*

U S.

1790 ■ *An Englishman named William Nicholson took out a patent for a cylinder printing press, but it was never built.*

The differences of thick and thin strokes in Baskerville's letters weren't as pronounced as one would suppose from the criticism he received. The lower case was similar to the amount of contrast found in the Caslon face. The differences in the individual types wouldn't necessarily have been noticed by many, but the differences in the books set in them was readily seen. Baskerville set his letters with generous spacing and leading, producing an open page, different from the page of his day. Also, the pages were simple and unornamented. [14]

It isn't true that open setting and deep spacing between lines were new, but he made these practices a consistent feature. So the difference wasn't a summer breeze; it was of sufficient force to bring about a general change in style which affected the appearance of the printed page for generations. It is a relevant point when one says that Baskerville's great influence upon typography arose from his use of wove paper and from his manner of using type, rather than from the design of his letters. [15]

His influence upon type design in England was apparent from the beginning, even though Modern type designs came to England from France and Italy, rather than as a development of Baskerville's Transitional face. Some of the leading founders of the late 1700s copied his designs, and his influence is seen in type designs of William Martin, brother of Robert Martin, Baskerville's apprentice and successor. Martin's fonts were displayed in the critically and financially successful publications of William Bulmer of the "Shakespeare Press" from 1791-1810.

ODE I.

AD VENEREM.

INTERMISSA, Venus

ella moves. Parce, p

Non sum qualis era

o Cinaræ. Desine, d

Mater sæva Cupidin

tra decem flectere m

Iam durum imperii

Type design used by Pierre Didot, 1799.

190

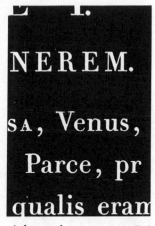

The evolution of type design from Old Style to Modern was, to some extent, related to technology. Mechanical improvements in the printing press and changes in the surface of paper permitted the engraver of types to create and reproduce designs that wouldn't have been possible earlier.

Most Modern type faces originated at the end of the eighteenth century and the beginning of the nineteenth century. Before then, the romain du roi of Philippe Grandjean, the typographic innovations of John Baskerville, and an interest in copperplate engraving exercised a considerable influence on type founders. What evolved were letters with: 1) greater contrast between the thick and thin strokes; 2) linear serifs NE which were straight and very fine (hairline); 3) a more narrow set; de and 4) a vertical emphasis.

The refinement and precision of Baskerville's type was little valued in England during his lifetime.

The design was Transitional, but it looked more Modern than it was. This was because of the sharpness of contrast made possible by his printing methods. Other type designers and printers in Europe appreciated his work, however, and his books influenced Giambattista Bodoni (1740-1813) in Italy, François Ambrose Didot (1730-1804) in Paris, and Joaquín Ibarra (1725-1785) in Madrid.

Quousque tan-
dem abutêre, Ca-
tilina , patientiâ
nostrâ? quamdiu
etiam furor iste
tuus nos eludet?
quem ad finem se-

Type designs from Bodoni's Manuale Tipografico, 1818.

The first of the Didot Family, which was famous in French printing in the 1800s, to become a type founder was F. A. Didot, known as l'aîne. He was printer by appointment to the king's brother. For the king (Louis XVI), he printed a collection of French authors. The type which was cut for him (by Waflard) was related to the design of Fournier, which was a variation on Grandjean's romain du roi. The presswork and ink were similar to Baskerville's, as was his papier vélin, a wove sheet he used. The Didot type imitated the engraver's tool; the light strokes became hairlines, and the serifs were unbracketed.[16]

des Peintures antiques de PIETRO-SAN

ns une seconde édition au public, parut

Paris, en 1757. Deux illustres savants, le

te, consacrerent les plus grands soins à

si intéressante, afin qu'elle répondît à la

ns la république des lettres.

ls en ouvrirent la souscription qu'elle

t seuls leur éloge, étoient trop imposants

: ne pas y obtenir un pareil succès. Nous

. le Beau, dans l'Éloge de M. le Comte

Bodoni was the son of a printer who, thoroughly trained in type cutting, typography, and printing, became royal book printer for the court of Ferdinand in Parma and remained there the rest of his life. When he began as a printer for the Duke of Parma, he used the letters and ornaments of Fournier. Then he made copies of his own; and, finally, he designed his own types in which the contrast was accentuated. The influence of his work, both his typographical style and presswork, was considerable. As a printer of books, he was highly regarded by the royal houses in Europe.

Italia, ch
diede il n
me al Go

e know not w

ere dawned u

1ich people u

ence, what be

om the big an

d all their ki

denote, unva

1at was the b

d most mome

Bodoni's designs weren't as condensed as those of Didot, although a reduction in the set of type had been anticipated. Didot's successors later

're en France pour le
ècle, c'est à bien peu
ier partout en Europe.
t point eu d'imitateurs

re-cut his Modern design in a condensed version.

Among Italian printers influenced by Bodoni and Didot was Andrea Amoretti, a former priest turned type designer, engraver, and printer. Although obscure, he cut and issued Modern faces

N'ayez de l'attac
l' amour pour
'à proportion du

in 1811 which were printed in Parma and Pisa. In many respects, they were well rendered.

LA GUERRA
DE JUGURTA
P O R
CAYO SALUSTIO CRISPO.

SIN *causa alguna se quexan los hombres de que su naturaleza es flaca y de corta duracion ; y que se govierna mas por la suerte , que por su virtud. Porque si bien se mira , se hallarà por el contrario, que no hai en el mundo cosa mayor , ni mas excelente ; y que no la falta vigor ni tiempo , si solo aplicacion e industria. Es pues la guia y el govierno entero de nuestra vida el animo ; el qual , si se encamina a la gloria por el sendero de la virtud , harto*

C. SALLUSTII CRISPI
IUGURTHA.

FALSO queritur de natura sua genus humanum , quod imbecille , atque ævi brevis, sorte potius , quam virtute , regatur. Nam contra reputando , neque majus aliud , neque præstabilius invenias ; magisque naturæ industriam hominum , quam vim , aut tempus deesse. Sed dux , atque imperator vitæ mortalium , animus est : qui ubi ad gloriam virtutis via grassa-

N

198

Joaquín Ibarra was Court Printer to Carlos III, an uncle to Ferdinand, who was Bodoni's royal patron. This Spanish printer was best known for his Sallust of 1772 and Don Quixote of 1780 in four volumes. Both were impressive editions. The typography was combined with many engraved illustrations on quality paper, and well printed. All details of the works were in Spanish. Like Baskerville, Ibarra experimented with ink and hot-pressed sheets of paper.

 usta cosa es que los hombres , que de-sean aventajarse a los demas vivien-tes , procuren con el mayor empeño no pasar la vida en silencio como las bestias , a quienes naturaleza criò in-clinadas a la tierra y siervas de su vientre. Nues-tro vigor y facultades consisten todas en el animo y el cuerpo² : de este usamos mas para el servicio , de aquel nos valemos para el mando : en lo uno somos iguales a los Dioses , en lo otro a los brutos. Por

C. SALLUSTII CRISPI
CATILINA.

veluti pecora ; quæ natura prona, atque ventri obedientia finxit. Sed nostra omnis vis in animo et cor–

Although Modern type designs have been criticized for use in bookwork and extended reading, they proved to be particularly effective, as well as for other forms of printing useful to the Industrial Revolution. They set a style which became popular in Europe and America and are still used extensively.

DISPLAY TYPES

From the time of the invention of movable type in the
early 1450s to the beginning of the nineteenth century,
display types—designed for use in commercial printing—
didn't exist. Till then printing was confined primarily
to the production of books. Printers used similar machines
and methods of production; their differences were judged
by the quality of their typography and printing. With
the Industrial Revolution in England and the need to
promote the sale of products, commercial printing grew.
Along came new and more complex equipment and the
demands of advertisers and other users of printed matter.
Newspaper and periodical printing developed, and
new styles of type were needed.

      The demand for commercial printing was related to
a basic change in manufacturing. Production concentrated
in those places where the raw materials, factories, machinery,
and workers existed. With this concentration there came into
being a need for better distribution of goods and better
ways to inform larger audiences that goods were for sale.

      In the graphic arts new processes, machines, and
equipment were introduced with great frequency.
Among these was a paper-producing machine invented
in 1803. In 1814 the first cylinder printing press,
which could produce 1,100 copies per hour, was printing
the London <u>Times</u>. Different kinds of typesetting machines
had been invented. The discovery of photography
had occurred.

Advertising had consisted largely of handbills and tradesmen's cards; the distribution and appeal of these were local. The advertising often told the public about the services of local craftsmen, not about specific products. Selling was largely an agreement between the persons who made the goods and the persons who needed them, and most products were individual in character; they were produced to individual order. In the early part of the Industrial Revolution, at least part of this way of doing business broke down, and the beginnings of new applications for printing came about.[17]

The different forms of advertising had different influences upon type designs but, perhaps, one of the most important was the poster. Early posters were set in a book style, using book faces in large sizes. Many such posters looked similar to title pages, though they usually contained more information. The layouts were essentially symmetrical and the weight or emphasis was often placed above the center of the page, though on a larger scale. But the range of type designs available at the end of the 1700s was limited.

Besides traditional type faces, several versions of Modern designs were generally available, as well as some which tended to be bolder; and there were blackletter faces. Type faces which were dissimilar in structure, such as Old Style and blackletter designs, were mixed frequently for contrast purposes. It became apparent that existing book types were inadequate for advertising, which needed large scale display and variation in emphasis. So for the first time, types were expected to call attention to themselves. Also, type faces became competitive for attention and were supposed to add an atmospheric overtone to the copy. Changes in type design took place in England in the early 1800s at a time when Transitional and Modern faces were fairly well established. There were, however, English books published at the end of the 1700s and in the early years of the nineteenth century which did not show a distinct change in type design. In 1795, William Bulmer printed a collection of poems by Goldsmith and Parnell. The type was Transitional in structure and many similar examples existed.

THE TRAVELLER.

Remote, unfriended, melancholy, slow,

Or by the lazy Scheld, or wandering Po;

Or onward, where the rude Carinthian boor

Against the houseless stranger shuts the door;

Or where Campania's plain forsaken lies,

A weary waste, expanding to the skies;

Where-e'er I roam, whatever realms to see,

THE TRAVELLER.

Remote, unfriended, melancholy, slow,
Or by the lazy Scheld, or wandering Po;
Or onward, where the rude Carinthian boor
Against the houseless stranger shuts the door;
Or where Campania's plain forsaken lies,
A weary waste, expanding to the skies;
Where-e'er I roam, whatever realms to see,
My heart, untravell'd, fondly turns to thee:
Still to my Brother turns, with ceaseless pain,
And drags at each remove a lengthening chain.

Generally, though, great changes were initiated in the faces of types of all kinds during the first years of the nineteenth century. The thick strokes were made thicker, and the fine lines retained their hairlines or were made finer. Ligatures were eliminated, and mechanical preciseness characterized some of the pages. At the same time, printers began to purchase "fancy founts of all degrees of grotesqueness," according to William Blades' <u>Early Type Specimen Books of England, Holland, France, Italy, and Germany</u>, published in London in 1875.

A preference in England, as in France, for very light faces began to change to heavier faces. The weight of these new faces was at first gained not by a greater weight of line throughout, but by thickening of the heavy strokes (stems) of letters. This left the thin strokes (hairlines) much as they were before in Modern designs.

1796 ■ Aloys Senefelder (a Bavarian) made relief etchings
on stone and metal plates. Further experiments led, in two years,
to a form of flat-surface printing called lithography.
■ A metal composing stick was invented by Hubert Rey in Lyons.

206

A first and obvious step, then,
in developing display faces was the
introduction of Modern letters rounded
in form and widened on the thick strokes,
mainly. Serifs were bracketed or slightly
bracketed, except on the hairlines,
which were always bracketed. These types,
which we now call **fat faces**, were first
displayed by the English typefounder
Thomas Cottrell in a specimen book of his
issued about 1765. More important,
through, they appeared regularly in his
specimen books after 1809. In time,
the designs were copied by other founders,

IL TO

whose letters tended to get bigger
and fatter.

The originator of **fat faces** was
Robert Thorne. He had been an apprentice
of Thomas Cottrell.

1798 ■ Nicolas Louis Robert (at the Essonnes mill owned by the Didot family)
invented a process for making paper in a continuous web.

Fat faces found immediate acceptance and were

soon followed by variations, **T** **R**

such as forward and backward sloping

italics, a shadow version **N**

with a third dimensional relief, and an inline

RE letter.

Their popularity diminished in the mid-1800s. It was not until the 1920s that their use was revived in the United States, as in the

ABCDEFGHIJKLM
abcdefghijklmnopqr

issuance of Ultra Bodoni, and in Germany.

1804 ■ Charles, Earl of Stanhope (of London) produced
a printing press constructed entirely of iron. It replaced
the hand presses made of wood. Both kinds operated on the
screw principle, but the design of Charles' contained a system
of compound levers that added to the power of the screw
on impression. It was given its first tests in the Bulmer
printing office. ■ Henry and Seeley Fourdrinier (in England)
perfected a machine (based on the Nicolas Louis Robert patent)
to make paper by passing pulp through rollers. The machine
increased the output of handmade paper by ten times.

e, wilt thou abuse

y frantic rage baffle

height meanest thou

Art thou nothing d

ecure the Palatium

ABCDEFGHIJKLMNOP
LMNOPQRSTUV

SQUARE SERIF TYPES

A second major development was a letterform called square serif. All the strokes of the letter were of a generally even thickness including

slab serifs, bracketed or **VE**

unbracketed. **N** In type specimen books

at the time, these characters were commonly called "Egyptian," for a reason that is unclear.
Square serif types were first shown by Vincent Figgins in his specimen book of 1817, under the name "Antique." Robert Thorne, who before his death in 1820 had cut several sizes and had set up specimens of them, named them "Egyptian" in the title line. The credit for designing them has never been established, but Figgins' specimen appeared several years before any other.

1810 ■ Frederick Koenig (König) built the first steam-driven
cylinder printing press. It was essentially an adaptation
of power to the hand press and was used, in a limited way,
for book printing. Later, Koenig and Andrew Bauer constructed
a flat-bed press with a continually revolving cylinder.
Two of the cylinder presses were built for the London Times
and powered by steam. It produced 1,100 impressions per hour,
greatly increasing the output of a hand press. Later, a press
was constructed to print on both sides of the sheet.
It was operated until 1827.

DEFGHI

The face came out originally in capitals only. The first lower-case design of square serif was issued later, in 1825, by the Caslon letter foundry. Then, italics and ornamented variations followed.

In 1845 a variation on the original square serif design, called Clarendon, was introduced.

bis vigiliæ,

This letter was from the Besley foundry in England. The letters, in upper and lower case, had a more narrow set, a noticeable difference between the thick and thin strokes, and

---

c. 1813 ■ George Clymer, working in Philadelphia and later in London (1817-34) built a printing press (The Columbian) that discarded the screw-raised platen, substituting a series of compound levers. Other iron presses used a kind of knuckle joint principle. The first was the press of John I. Wells of Hartford (1891), which was superseded by the Washington hand press of Samuel Rost of New York (1821).

bracketed serifs. Although this wasn't the first such type design produced during this period, it was extensively copied after the three-year copyright had expired. The type style was used in a variety of sizes, as well as extended and condensed versions.

Square serif faces were revived in the

1920s **Er** and 1950s.

In the twenties and thirties, thick and thin strokes were now lacking, though; the letters were of even weight, unbracketed, and geometric.

beliebt ist.

The letters, such as Memphis, produced about 1930 in Germany, reflected efforts at the time to simplify letterforms. The revived faces of the fifties were related to the original Clarendon and Ionic designs.

**to denote, unvaryingly, certain sounds?
That was the birth of the alphabet, one of
and most momentous triumphs of the hu**

1822 ■ J. N. Niepce produced the first photomechanical
printing plate. He etched a reproduction of an engraving on a
sensitized metal plate. ■ The Rosetta stone was deciphered.
■ A type casting machine was patented in England by Dr. William
Church of Boston. The device was capable of producing 3,000
individual pieces of type in an hour.

HISTOIRE

DE

LOUIS DE BOURBON,

SECOND DU NOM,

PRINCE

DE CONDÉ,

PREMIER PRINCE DU SANG,

Surnommé LE GRAND.

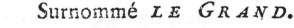

1827 ■ Two engineers for the London Times built a cylinder press which printed on one side of the sheet. It permitted 4,000 impressions per hour. It was used until 1848 when it was replaced by a press with cylinders in a vertical position; the type was held in place by wedge-shaped column rules. This press printed 8,000 impressions per hour.

DECORATIVE TYPES

In the early 1800s letters in Britain began
to be modified in form by being condensed,
expanded, outlined, etc., and/or they were
decorated on their faces. Most decorative faces
produced then, of which there were many, were
a response to the demands of commercial printers,
rather than book printers. Early shadowed
or three-dimensional letters (1819-21) were
fat faces. They were white faces outlined
in black with a black shadow.
They came in a variety of sizes
in capitals, some in italics.

Decorative type faces weren't
entirely new, though. They had been fairly
popular in France and the Low Countries
in the eighteenth century. For instance,
Pierre Simon Fournier produced modified

inline letters in his <u>Manuel</u>

<u>Typographique</u> in 1764, and decorative
capitals in 1768.

Before type founding, decorative letters appeared in Italian Renaissance calligraphy and earlier still, in the manuscripts of scribes.

The faces of British types of this time were often decorated, too. At first the open areas of letters were filled in with a linear pattern

RBU or decoration.

Later, both the face and the form of the letter became decorative, as with Tuscans.

In the first half of the century, British typefounders led in the creation and production of decorative job types. The faces were widely used and copied in Europe and America, as well. Besides embellished and shadowed or three-dimensional type faces, British foundries sold outline or open types, inlines, rounded letters, and cameo or reversed faces. True outline letters, such as the sample

from the Figgins foundry in 1833,

had a reasonably consistent weight line which enclosed the shape of the letter. Some open letters had outlines which were slightly heavier on one side, like this Blake & Stephenson design

NITURE

of about 1833, but not as heavy on one side
as to approach the look of a shadowed face.
Inlines, in their pure form, had the appearance
of having a white line drawn on the strokes

of the letter. Rounded letters were

essentially sans serifs with rounded terminals.
The earliest reversed faces were white fat faces,
square serifs, or Tuscans on what looked like
a continuous black
(solid) background;
there weren't visible
joins to adjoining
letters. When they had a modest revival
in the 1920s and 30s, letters next to one another

were separated by a vertical, white

(negative) line. They often had a patterned

background (cameo).

1829 ■ Claude Gerroux, a French printer, introduced the
papier-mache matrix for stereotyping. ■ The first U.S. patent
on a typewriter was granted to William Burt of Detroit.

The typefounders who issued fat faces, square serif, and

decorative fonts in the early 1800s said they were meant

for printing handbills and other job printing, rather

than book work. Nevertheless, traditional types were

shown and used rarely during this period in England.

There were exceptions, of course–primarily with

the newly-founded private presses. William Pickering,

for example, turned back to the type designs

of the fifteenth and sixteenth centuries. Also, he was

an early participant in the separation of book design

from printing. He published a number of well-received

books and, with Charles Whittingham of the Chiswick

1839 ■ Photography became a practical process
because of the work of Louis J. Daguerre of France
and W. H. Fox Talbot of England.
1843 ■ Friedrich Keller, a Saxon weaver, manufactured paper
from wood pulp. Within ten years, the process spread
throughout Europe and the United States.
1847 ■ The first rotary press, manufactured by Richard M. Hoe
of New York, was installed by the Philadelphia Public Ledger.
It ran 8,000 sheets an hour, printed on one side.
1852 ■ W. H. Fox Talbot invented photogravure on steel plates.
1853 ■ The offset method of printing was patented
by John Strather of England. An early practical application
came in the 1870s, when rubber offset rollers were used
on flat bed presses for printing on tin and other metals.

Press, resurrected Caslon Old Face in 1844.

In Germany, typefounders issued traditional designs, also, and many new faces including Moderns, scripts, and blackletter. The private presses there, for which newly commissioned proprietary typefaces were often cut, prospered later on–from the early 1900s to the mid-thirties. Many of the type designs have survived, including the faces of Weiss, Koch,

1852–77 ■ Experiments were conducted to discover a means for breaking up continuous tones of photographs and drawings, to produce printed images in black and white.
1854 ■ The curved casting box for making stereotypes was developed, making possible printing by rotary presses.
1856 ■ The earliest patent that referred to a phototypesetting machine was granted in England.
1859–62 ■ The first attempts at photoengravings (etched metal printing plates) were made in England, France, Austria, and Czechoslovakia. Photography wasn't used originally; the images on the plates were drawn or lithographic transfers were employed.
1861 ■ Clerk Maxwell, an English physicist, published the theory of color reproduction (by means of three-color light filters).

Bernhard, and Renner.

Books published by the French private presses

at the time tended to be generously illustrated with

wood engravings and lithographs. The formats were often

less formal, which reflected a break from neoclassicism,

and may have invited unfair criticism of the books,

generally, as being typographically inferior.

1862 ■ Halftone plates for letterpress printing
were shown at a London exhibition.
1865 ■ The first steam-driven lithographic press
was perfected by Hughes and Kimber in England.
It was introduced into the United States in 1866.
1873 ■ H. W. Vogel discovered optical sensitization,
which led to the reproduction of color copy in monochrome
by use of orthochromatic plates.
1878 ■ American point system introduced by John Marder.
1884 ■ Linn Boyd Benton, an American type founder,
patented a pantographic punch-cutting machine.
The invention helped make mechanical composition practicable;
it could engrave any number of identical punches
from a mechanical drawing.
1907 ■ Samuel Simon of Manchester, England, received a patent
for the silk screen process of printing.
1910 ■ The percentage cost of paper for book production
was about seven percent. In 1740 it had been as high
as twenty percent.
1915 ■ A. E. Bawtree phototypesetter, presumably influenced
by an 1856 British patented machine, was introduced. The device
used a negative disc with rings of characters around its circumference.
1919 ■ The Dulton Photo-Line phototypesetting device was built.
It was made up of two separate units; one was a lettersetting machine,
the other was a camera.

de l'amitié, se réveillaient dans leur âme, une religion pure, aidée par des mœurs chastes, les dirigeaient vers une autre vie, comme la flamme qui s'envole vers le ciel, lorsqu'elle n'a plus d'aliment sur la terre.

SANS SERIF FACES

Fat faces, square serifs, and decorative
letters were soon joined by a new type
design, sans serif–a letter without serifs
in which all the strokes were of a fairly
even thickness. This was in a sense
a development without precedent in type
design. Whether the designs were inspired
by early Greek stone inscriptions or not
is unknown, though it seems remote.
We do know that ancient capital letters were
without serifs. The Romans may have added serifs
to clean off the strokes of the chisel, or
as a finishing stroke, or as an aid to reading.
Nonetheless, letters without serifs continued
to appear throughout history in modified forms,
especially as carved letters on buildings
and coins.

It should be remembered that
the sans serif design–or any "new" type
design–wasn't really an invention;
it was an adaptation of what was known.
The basic letter shapes were established
long before. So while it was possible
to modify the shapes, it wasn't possible
to create original letters.

A sans serif design was introduced
into metal type in 1816. William Caslon IV,
descendant of the English type founder, showed

CASLON

a single size (two-line English size) in capitals
under the name "Egyptian."

The design was published again
in about 1819 and later, in 1838 by a second
English type foundry, but it seems this face was
never used. In 1830, Figgins' specimen sheets
showed a heavier version called "sans-serif."

WITH
USEH

In 1830, Thorowgood's heavy, relatively
condensed alphabet, called "Grotesque,"

was offered with a lower-case design.
Outlined, shadowed, and ornamented variations
followed. During this period, the 1830s,
the sans serif design gained more attention,
and its use spread to Europe, particularly
Germany, and to some extent, the United States.

Beside being heavy and black, most of the
early sans serifs were issued in capitals only,
with letters of uniform width. Lighter cuttings
came later. In the 1847 Figgins' specimen book,
there was a large series of sans serif faces
in different sizes. One in particular was lighter

SONDE

and, though slightly expanded, the widths were
more normal. Aside from some problems, perhaps,

with the loops in a few letters, such as **P**

and **R**, the design was immediately copied

by other founders. By 1860, the basic letterform –
a lighter, open rendering – was displayed
in almost all specimen books in England. The
use of lower case appears to have been used
in England more often after the 1870s, but
in Germany and the United States (where the
design was called grotesk and gothic,
respectively), sans serifs with lower case
were in use earlier.

The early sans serif was a square serif face

with the serifs removed, and it may be that this is how

it was created. Its weight was easily altered without,

in some cases, basically changing the particular type

design. This gave the letter a plastic quality.

1922 ■ The Robertson PhotoLinotype appeared.
It used a converted line caster and larger than normal
matrices. A camera and film unit replaced the metal casting unit.
At first the character images were positioned on the matrix edge
and light was reflected from them. Later, the matrices
were redesigned with glass character negatives
mounted on metal frames. The Smothers Phototypesetter of 1925
was a similiar machine, but the negative character images
were imbedded in glass on the edge of the matrix.

Similarly, height to width relationships, unlike roman

designs, were more flexible. This led, by 1900,

to the development of a type family—a particular

sans serif type design in different weights and sets:

for example, News Gothic, issued in 1908. This and other

ABCDEFGHIJKLMNOPQRSTU\
abcdefghijklmnopqrstuvwxyz

family faces were designed for both display and text

settings. Unlike earlier types, the designs were now

drawn on larger scales, altered for optical considerations

created by changes to different point sizes, and

photographically reduced to various point sizes.

The use of sans serif faces declined
during the first two decades of the twentieth
century. In the 1920s a number of serifless types
was reintroduced. Most of the letters were
geometric, rendered in strokes which had a
visually even thickness. They reflected efforts
to simplify letters, to relate the shapes—
often based on roman proportions—to function.

annot guess

d the fact th

ressed by a f

o select

ss of ideogr

ber of signs

sounds?

abet, one of t

s of the hum

One of the most popular faces was Futura,
designed in 1927 as a book face by Paul Renner,
former director of the Munich School of Design.

Futura Medium (Bauer)
ABCDEFGHIJKLMNOPQRSTU'
XYZ abcdefghijklmnopqrstuvv
1234567890

Technical developments in the graphic arts
and throughout society, which accelerated
during this time, encouraged new views
not only about the shapes of letters but
the forms on pages, too. The adaptation
of principles related to various movements
in the visual arts had an effect
on the division of space by means of
geometric forms. There was now a reliance
on rectangles, circles, and straight lines
ordered in an asymmetric arrangement—
a planned deviation from a classical
structure. In a general sense, there was
a simplicity of line and a formal

geometricity to the pages, to express, among other things, the industrial character then. It also seemed that emotion, at least in its outward appearance and except in a purely aesthetic sense, played a secondary role. In this light, Futura, and the way it was used, represented the period.

Another was Sans Serif, designed in the early 1930s by Sol Hess for the Lanston Monotype Machine Company. It was offered in light, medium, bold, and extra bold versions. Less heralded than Futura, its letters were beautifully proportioned–in the light version, for example–and closely fit. They looked warmer and seemed less concerned with mirroring the world of technology.

abcdefghijklmnopqrstuvwxyz

abcdefghijklmnopqrstuvwxyz

ABCDEFG HIJKLM

The same might be said for Gill Sans.

We know not when, and we cannot guess whei
there dawned upon some mind the fact that all
which people uttered are expressed by a few s
Hence, what better plan than to select
from the big and confused mass of ideograms,
and all their kin, a certain number of signs
to denote, unvaryingly, certain sounds?
That was the birth of the alphabet, one of the g
and most momentous triumphs of the human m

Edward Clod

It appeared in the late 1920s and was used
extensively during the 30s and 40s. Soon after
it was issued, its success prompted weight and

set variations, including **extra bold**
ultra bold , and **bold condensed** .

As with most variants on medium weight, geometric
sans serifs, the adaptations didn't always relate
well to the original design; the shapes often
seemed strained.

1946 ■ The first field tests were made of the Intertype Fotosetter.
In the same year, Lithomat Company entered into an agreement
with Rene Alphonse Higonnet and Louis Marius Moyroud, which led
to the development of the Photon typesetter.

We know not when, and we cannot g
there dawned upon some mind the fː
which people uttered are expressed l
Hence, what better plan than to sel
from the big and confused mass oſ
and all their kin, a certain number ͼ
to denote, unvaryingly, certain souı
That was the birth of the alphabet, one o
and most momentous triumphs of the hu
We know not when, and we canno
there dawned upon some mind thͼ
which people uttered are expresse
Hence, what better plan than to se
from the big and confused mass oˀ
and all their kin, a certain number of siɡ
to denote, unvaryingly, certain sounds?
That was the birth of the alphabet, one ͼ
and most momentous triumphs of the hu
We know not when, and we cannc
there dawned upon some mind thͼ
which people uttered are expre
Hence, what better plan than tc
from the big and confused mas
and all their kin, a certain numl

Univers digital type face design. Mergenthaler Linotype Stempel Haas.

232

In the 1950s the various designs within a sans serif type family were integrated more successfully, particularly in Univers. The Univers family, designed originally for phototypesetting by Adrian Frutiger, a Swiss type designer, contained twenty-one variations of the design. They ranged from light weights to extra bold versions, in varying widths and italics.[18] The design approach was followed by other firms, which produced well designed, integrated variants, such as Folio and Helvetica.

In recent years, the number of readily producible modifications of a sans serif, or any other type face design, increased dramatically. This came about through the use of phototypesetters and digital typesetters with extended machine

---

1950 ■ The Intertype Fotosetter was exhibited
at a printing exposition in Chicago. The Fotosetter
used a matrix (Fotomat) similar to a linecaster matrix,
but with a negative character image imbedded in its center.
The machine, which resembled a linecaster, had a camera
in place of the casting mechanism. Although more than sixty patents
for photocomposition devices had been issued in the preceding
fifty years, this was the first one to be marketed.
1955 ■ The Monophoto phototypesetter was issued.
Since it was based on the same principles as the Monotype,
it was a first generation machine, like the Fotosetter.
c.1957 ■ Relief printing plates created by photographic methods,
such as magnesium or acetate "etched" plates and photopolymer plates,
began to be used.
1958 ■ The Mergenthaler Linotype Company first demonstrated in
Europe their "Linofilm" at DRUPA, the internatonal printing exhibition
held at Dusseldorf.

We know no

there dawne

which peopl

Hence, what

from the big

and all their

to denote, ur

That was the

and most mc

Enlargement of 12 point Optima digital type face design.

capabilities. Additional variations could include inline, outline, shadow, oblique, condensed, and expanded letters, obtainable in different degrees and combinations.

In a like manner, current technology is being applied to designing new typefaces. As seen in the work of Donald Knuth, a mathematician and computer scientist at Stanford University, it is possible to draw letters with a computer "to

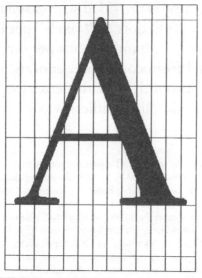

1960 ■ The initial design of a ruby laser (light amplification by stimulated emission of radiation) was developed, based on work originally done in 1958 at Bell Laboratories.
1962 ■ IBM and RCA supplied hyphenation-justification programs for photocomposition based on general-purpose computers. It was adopted mainly by newspapers at first; book production came a little while later.
1967 ■ A prototype of the Linotron 505, an early third generation photocomposition device, was shown at DRUPA.

imitate the calligrapher who uses pen and ink."[19]

Using a software program and certain terminals and other devices, the operator explains how a letter is to look. The final design is solved by finding a mathematical way to define shapes of letters and by converting them to the smallest unit of information in a computer.

Each letter is displayed on a screen (cathode ray tube), which scans 1000 lines per inch. So the operator is provided with a square grid pattern with 1000 dots or "pixels" per linear inch and in which, at 30 million bits per second, points are plotted from complex equations. The operator can see instantly how the letter looks, and, of course, modify it in endless ways.

1968 ■ Compugraphic Corp. introduced a line of spinning-font phototypesetters at prices below $10,000. Some included, for the first time, an internal ability to justify and hyphenate by hard-wired logic. It marked the beginning of the wide use of phototype.

1970 ■ Harris Corp. introduced the 1100 "stand-alone" video editing terminal for correcting and revising text on Teletypesetter (punched paper) tape. ■ CompuScan, Inc. exhibited an OCR (optical character recognition) device for typesetting text input applications. Earlier OCR devices were applied to reading numeric information printed on credit card slips.

1971 ■ Hendrix Electronics offered one of the first on-line (tapeless) packaged compostion systems, for use in newspaper and periodical production, which integrated text input and editing terminals and phototypesetter under central computer control.

1972 ■ Harris showed 2200 terminals, called a Video Layout System, for CRT visualization and keyboard control of layouts for newspaper display advertisements. It displayed an approximation of actual type sizes, faces, and positions.

The system is a unique and provocative application of design principles advanced and rendered during the Italian Renaissance (by Fellice Feliciano and Leonardo da Vinci), and which were put to use by the Academie des Sciences in 1692, and by Geoffroy Tory later on. As such, it serves as a reminder that the development of letterforms has been long, slow, and erratic, with more than intermittent revivals. As a march, from the pictograms of the caves and into the syllabic writing of settled encampments, growing into the alphabetic writing of city-states and the letters of nations, it has been triumphant. In that light, our status today is merely a way station.

1974 ■ Raytheon delivered the Raycomp system for computer-aided interactive production of typography for newspaper display ads. Outputs were by way of any of several CRT phototypesetters.
1975-80 ■ Several firms offered "word processing printers" which generated type images to produce composed text, usually at or below minimum graphic arts quality. Various mechanical, laser, and CRT methods were used, including ink-jet printing.
1976 ■ Numerous U. S. newspapers installed combined "on-line" input, editing, and typesetting systems which used general-purpose computer and disk mass storage. Most advertising and page make-up remained a separate function, however.
1979 ■ R. L. White Co., Louisville, installed the Information International, Inc. system for storing and retrieving halftones in digitized form. The output of both halftones and typography was via a large CRT typesetting machine.
1979-80 ■ Mergenthaler and Compugraphic introduced "electrographic" phototypesetters which produced an image on a surface other than a silver photographic one, using electrostatic imaging.

REFERENCES CITED
IN THE INTRODUCTION

1. Daniel Berkeley Updike,
   Printing Types, Their History, Forms, and Use, Vol. I
   (Cambridge: Harvard University Press, 1937), pp. 38-40.

2. I. J. Gelb,
   A Study of Writing
   (Chicago: The University of Chicago Press, 1963), pp. 35-36.

3. Hans Jensen,
   Sign, Symbol and Script
   (New York: G. P. Putnam's Sons, 1969), p. 50.

4. J. Hambleton Ober,
   Writing: Man's Great Invention
   (Baltimore: The Peabody Institute, 1965), pp. 37-38.

5. Ibid., pp. 38-42.

REFERENCES CITED
IN PART I

1. Jensen, p. 87.

2. Ober, pp. 55-56.

3. Edward Clodd,
   The Story of the Alphabet
   (Detroit: Gale Research Company, 1970), p. 99.

4. Jensen, p. 96.

5. Ober, pp. 56-57.

6. Jensen, p. 59.

7. Keith Gordon Irwin,
   The Romance of Writing

(New York: The Viking Press, 1956), pp. 34-35

8. Gelb, p. 129.

9. Ober, p. 102.

10. Ibid., p. 108.

REFERENCES CITED IN PART II

1. Clodd, pp. 213-215.

2. Jensen, p. 453.

3. Ober, pp. 116-117.

4. Irwin, pp. 52-56.

5. Gelb, p. 184

6. Horst de la Croix and Richard G. Tansey,
   Gardner's Art through the Ages
   (New York: Harcourt, Brace & World, Inc., 1970), pp. 174-176.

REFERENCES CITED IN PART III

1. Updike, Vol. I, p. 42.

2. Frederic W. Goudy,
   The Alphabet and Elements of Lettering
   (New York: Dover Publications, Inc., 1963), p. 43.

3. Jensen, p. 551.

4. Ibid., p. 533.

5. Alexander Nesbitt,

The History and Technique of Lettering
(New York: Dover Publications, Inc., 1957), p. 23.

6. Ibid, p. 22.

7. Jacques Boussard,
The Civilization of Charlemagne
(New York: McGraw-Hill Book Co., 1968), p. 118.

8. Ibid., pp. 121-124.

9. Peter Munz,
Life in the Age of Charlemagne
(London: B.T. Batsford Ltd., 1969), p. 112.

10. F.L. Ganshof,
The Carolingians and the Frankish Monarchy
(Ithaca: Cornell University Press, 1971), p. 30.

11. Boussard, pp. 126-127.

12. Donald Bullough,
The Age of Charlemagne
(London: Paul Elek Ltd., 1973), p. 115.

13. Ibid., p. 115.

14. Boussard, pp. 130-131.

15. Bullough, p. 118.

REFERENCES CITED IN PART IV

1. Geoffrey Dowding,
An Introduction to the History of Printing Types
(London: Wace & Company Ltd., 1961), p. 87.

2. Nesbitt, p. 98.

3. Erik Lindegren,

ABC of Lettering and Printing Types
(New York: Museum Books Inc., 1965), C. p. 80.

4. Talbot Baines Reed,
A History of the Old English Letter Foundries
(London: Faber and Faber Limited, 1952), p. 235.

5. Allen Hutt,
Fournier, the Compleat Typographer
(Totowa, N.J.: Rowman and Littlefield, 1972), p. 7.

6. Stanley Morison,
Type Design of the Past and Present
(London: The Fleuron, Limited, 1926), p. 36.

7. Updike, Vol.II. p. 107.

8. Josiah Henry Benton,
John Baskerville
(New York: Burt Franklin, 1968), p. 3.

9. F.E. Pardoe,
John Baskerville of Birmingham
(London: Frederick Muller Limited, 1975), p. 11.

10. W. Turner Berry and H. Edmond Poole,
Annals of Printing
(Toronto: University of Toronto Press, 1966), p. 169.

11. Phillip Gaskell,
John Baskerville, A Bibliography
(Cambridge: Cambridge University Press, 1959), p. xxi.

12. Ibid., p. xx.

13. Benton, pp. 35-36.

14. Lawrence C. Wroth,
A History of the Printed Book
(New York: The Limited Editions Club, 1938), p. 219.

15. Ibid., p. 219

16. Updike, Vol. I, pp 216-217.

17. Raymond Roberts,
    Typographic Design
    (London: Ernest Benn Limited, 1966), pp. 19-20.

18. Alexander Lawson,
    Printing Types: An Introduction
    (Boston: Beacon Press, 1971). pp. 99-101.

19. Donald E. Knuth,
    Tex and Metafont, New Directions in Typesetting
    (Bedford, Mass.: Digital Press and the American
    Mathematical Society, 1979), 1 p. 27.

OTHER REFERENCES

■ E. M. Almedingen
Charlemagne, a Study
    (London: The Bodley Head Ltd., 1968).

■ Roland Baughman and Robert O. Schad
Great Books in Great Editions
    (San Marino, Ca.: The Huntington Library, 1965).

■ E. C. Bigmore and C. W. H. Wyman
A Bibliography of Printing
    (New York: Philip C. Duschnes, 1945).

■ Joseph Blumenthal
Art of the Printed Book 1455–1955
    (New York: The Pierpont Morgan Library, 1978).

■ J. Bronowski
The Ascent of Man
    (Boston: Little, Brown and Co., 1973).

■ Harry Carter
A View of Early Typography
    (Oxford: Clarendon Press, 1969).

■ Warren Chappell
The Living Alphabet
   (Charlottesville: The University Press of Virginia, 1975).

■ Colin Clair
A History of Printing in Britain
   (New York: Oxford University Press, 1965).

■ Theo. L. De Vinne
Historic Printing Types
   (New York: The Grolier Club, 1886).

■ Eleanor Shipley Duckett
Carolingian Portraits
   (Ann Arbor: The University of Michigan Press, 1962).

■ Early Printed Books
   (New York: The Pierpont Morgan Library, 1974).

■ Stewart C. Easton and Helen Wieruszowski
The Era of Charlemagne
   (Princeton: D. Van Nostrand Company, Inc., 1961).

■ Heinrich Fichtenau
The Carolingian Empire
   (Oxford: Basil Blackwell, 1963).

■ Cyrus H. Gordon
Forgotten Scripts
   (New York: Basic Books, Inc., 1968).

■ Chandler B. Grannis, ed.
Heritage of the Graphic Arts
   (New York: R. R. Bowker Co., 1972).

■ Michael Grant
The Etruscans
   (New York: Charles Scribner's Sons, 1980).

■ Nicolete Gray
Nineteenth Century Ornamental Typefaces
   (Berkeley and Los Angeles: University of California Press, 1976).

■ T.C. Hansard
Typographia
(London: Baldwin, Cradock, and Joy, 1825).

■ Stanley C. Hlasta
Printing Types and How to Use Them
(Pittsburgh: Carnegie Press, 1950).

■ R. S. Hutchings
A Manual of Decorated Typefaces
(New York: Hastings House Publishers, 1965).

■ Donald Jackson
The Story of Writing
(New York: Taplinger Publishing Co., Inc., 1981).

■ H. W. Janson
A Basic I Iistory of Art
(Englewood Cliffs, N.J.: Prentice-Hall, Inc., 1971).

■ Douglas C. McMurtrie
The Book
(New York: Covici, Fricde, Publishers, 1937).

■ A. Hyatt Mayor
Prints & People
(New York: The Metropolitan Museum of Art, 1971).

Mediaeval & Renaissance Manuscripts
(New York: The Pierpont Morgan Library, 1974).

■ Stanley Morison
Four Centuries of Fine Printing
(New York: Barnes & Noble Inc., 1960).

■ Stanley Morison
LetterForms
(London: Nattali & Maurice, 1968).

Realites Treasures of the Louvre
(New York: G. P. Putnam's Sons, 1966).

■ Laurence Scarfe

Alphabets
    (London: B. T. Batsford Ltd., 1954).

■ John W. Seybold
Fundamentals of Modern Composition
    (Media, Pa.: Seybold Publications, Inc., 1977).

■ John K. Standish and Arnold Bank
The Origin of Type Designs and The Garamond Story
    (Portland: Portland Club of Printing House Craftsmen, 1955).

■ S. H. Steinberg
Five Hundred Years of Printing
    (Baltimore: Penguin Books, 1969).

■ Walter Ullman
The Carolingian Renaissance and the Idea of Kingship
    (London: Methuen & Co., Ltd., 1969).

■ Herman Zapf
About Alphabets
    (Cambridge: The M. I. T. Press, 1970).

I N D E X

D

S

T